RAYLEIGH PARISH

FIRE BRIGADE RU

CONSTITUTION.

The Brigade shall be called " The Rayleigh Fire Brigade " and shall consist of a Captain, Second Officer, Engineer and four firemen.

ELECTION OF MEMBERS.

The Captain, Second Officer and Engineer shall be appointed by the Parish Council and be responsible to that body. Firemen (when a vacancy occurs) shall be elected by the votes of a majority of the members present at a Meeting of the Brigade, each election being subject to the confirmation of the Fire Brigade Committee of the Parish Council.

CANDIDATES FOR MEMBERSHIP.

Applicants for membership of the Brigade must be of good character and physique. On appointment each fireman must attend at least six drills before being provided with uniform ; three months probation. Applicants must address their applications to the Captain in the first instance. Firemen are required to retire at the age of 65 years.

NEW MEMBERS.

Each Member on joining shall subscribe his name to the Rules and Regulations of the Brigade in a book kept for that purpose, and shall be furnished with a copy of these rules so that ignorance of the conditions under which he serves cannot be pleaded.

UNIFORM.

All Members of the Brigade shall be provided with uniform, which shall consist of helmet, undress cap, tunic, trousers, boots, lifeline, belt, axe and case. These shall be provided by the Council without cost to the member and shall remain the property of the Council. Firemen will be held responsible for their uniform and will be required to keep them clean and in good repair, and on leaving the Brigade must at once deliver up such uniform and implements. Uniform may only be worn on duty, or on special authority of the Captain.

RESIDENCE OF MEMBERS.

On changing their address Members must at once notify the Captain ; any Member leaving the town for more than 24 hours must notify the Captain, so that his absence may be understood at either Fires or Drills.

RETIREMENT FROM MEMBERSHIP.

Any Member wishing to retire from the Brigade shall give 28 days' notice to the Captain in writing.

DRILLS.

There shall be at least one uniform drill each month, and such additional drills as shall be considered necessary by the Captain. Each Member shall put in no less than 12 drills each year. A Register shall be kept by the Captain of the attendance at Drills of each Member.

DISCIPLINE.

When at Fires or Drills the orders of the Captain or Senior Officer must be unquestionably obeyed without delay. At Fires the Chief Officer has complete control of all operations in connection with the extinguishing of the outbreak of fire in which the Brigade is engaged.

By order of the

Parish Council.

CHAS. E. JUDD,

Clerk

18th June 1928.

RAYLEIGH
A History

RAYLEIGH
A History

Ian Yearsley

Phillimore

2005

Published by
PHILLIMORE & CO. LTD
Shopwyke Manor Barn, Chichester, West Sussex, England

© Ian Yearsley, 2005

ISBN 1 86077 355 9

Printed and bound in Great Britain by
CAMBRIDGE PRINTING

*This book is dedicated
to the memory of
Philip Benton, historian of the Rochford Hundred,
whose writings and researches
have frequently informed my own.*

*Also to those suffering from
Repetitive Strain Injury (RSI).
Rest, research, adapt.
You will get through it.*

Contents

List of Illustrations

Frontispiece: Rayleigh Church and windmill from Rayleigh Mount.

Acknowledgements

First and foremost, I would like to thank my wife Alison for her practical assistance with the research and writing of this book and for her on-going help and support in this and many other aspects of my life.

Secondly, I would like to thank Noel Osborne and colleagues at Phillimore & Co. Ltd for the faith they have shown in me in asking me to write this book and for the patience and understanding they have shown throughout its research and writing.

Many people provided invaluable assistance with the research, including in particular the staff at the Southend and Chelmsford branches of the Essex Record Office, especially the ladies at the former who put in a lot of time to locate and provide relevant documents, and Ken Crowe at Southend Museums Service who made time to make available to me many old photographs of old Rayleigh. My thanks also go to Richard Harris and Jennifer Butler at the Essex Record Office for granting me permission to use various illustrations from the collections there and to staff at Colchester Library for their help with locating documents. Thanks also to staff at Rochford Library and to Margaret Saunders at Rayleigh Town Council.

I would also like to thank Ann and Derek Jolly, Janet Connors and colleagues at Rayleigh Library, Susan Gough/Southend Library, Ruarigh Dale and Trevor Ennis of the Essex County Council Field Archaeology Unit and Edward Clack for providing photographs and related information on various aspects of Rayleigh's history, and Oliver Rackham for giving me permission to use illustrations from his book *The Woods of South East Essex*. Also to Sarah Ward of the Essex Police Museum for providing and granting me permission to use photographs from the museum's collection and to the British Library for giving permission to reproduce the picture of Hubert de Burgh.

Also of assistance were the Rayleigh local historians Noel Beer, Ernie Lane and Mike Davies, plus Norman Grant and colleagues at The Historical Society of Rayleigh, Michael Stone of the National Trust Local Committee, Kenneth Gee of the Rayleigh Civic Society, Jeremy Lamb of The Field Lane Foundation and Sonia Worthington and Helen Collins of Rochford District Council, plus Martin Bashforth of the National Railway Museum and Alan Osborne of the Essex Bus Enthusiasts Group.

Also members of the Salvation Army and the ministers, churchwardens and congregations of various Rayleigh churches, including Holy Trinity (Rev. Parrott/ Ann Jolly/Joyce Edmonds), the Baptist Church (Rev. Jerry Brown), the Methodist Church, the United Reformed Church (Rev. Birgit Brophy) and the Catholic Church (Father Andrew Dorricott).

The illustrations in this book are reproduced by courtesy of the following: Noel Beer, 155; British Library, 10; Edward Clack, 1, 15, 144, 151; Essex County Council; 7; Essex Police Museum, 138-9; Essex Record Office, front endpaper (Fire Brigade Rules), 22, 26, 40, 83-5, 87, 91, 98-9, 101, 107, 109, 116-7, 121-3, 130, 132-3; Ann Jolly, 51; Ann Jolly/the rector and churchwardens of Holy Trinity Church, 95; Phillimore & Co. Ltd, 65, 73, 126; Oliver Rackham, 16-17; Rayleigh Library, endpapers, 47, 76, 89, 110, 127, 129, 145-6; Rochford District Council, 49; Southend Library, 24; and Southend Museums Service, 2-6, 8-9, 13, 27, 29-30, 45-6, 50, 54-5, 57, 59-60, 63, 66, 71, 77, 88, 92, 96, 103. All efforts have been made to trace the copyright holders for 128 and 143. If either of these illustrations is still within copyright I apologise to all concerned. All other pictures are from the author's collection.

One

Introduction and Early History

❖

The story of Rayleigh begins with its geography.

In the otherwise flat and low-lying area of south-east Essex in which the town is located, the ridge of hills on which Rayleigh grew up was an obvious place to investigate for the first human explorers. This ridge, which rises some 200 feet and runs for just over five miles from the south-west at South Benfleet to the north-east at Hockley, offered the prospect of both an excellent vantage point over the surrounding countryside and a base for an easily defensible encampment. At either end of the ridge is a river (the Thames to the south, the Crouch to the north), a key artery of the transport network for early man.

Rayleigh lies just to the north of the centre of the ridge, at its narrowest here and with good vantage points all round, particularly to the north and west, and with fairly easy access to both rivers and the River Roach, a tributary of the Crouch. The town's central position on the ridge has led to the latter being known as the 'Rayleigh Hills'.

1 An aerial view of modern Rayleigh, showing the prospect over the fields towards the River Crouch. The importance of the location as a good, defensible vantage point was a major factor in the early settlement of the hilltop town.

2   Hambro Hill, *c*.1911. It was to the top of this hill in the Stone Age that the first human visitors to Rayleigh came. This is one of a number of photographs in this book from the lens of Alfred Padgett, a prolific local photographer whose collection is now in the care of Southend Museums Service.

Despite subsequent development in the centuries since the area was first settled, modern-day visitors can still testify to the fine views that can be had over the surrounding countryside and the landmarks on the skyline that the town's buildings provide. Basildon new town, Rettendon church, the River Crouch, South Woodham Ferrers, Cold Norton water tower and even Danbury church, some ten miles away, can all be seen from vantage points in the town. Hockley, Rayleigh and Thundersley churches, Rayleigh windmill and the water towers at Hockley, Thundersley and South Benfleet are all major local landmarks on the Rayleigh Hills.

One of the best views of Rayleigh's hilltop skyline to be had locally is from Sweyne Park, to the north-west of the town centre off Victoria Avenue between London Road and Rawreth Lane.

STONE AGE

The earliest evidence for the human occupation of Rayleigh comes from the Stone Age (principally the Middle Stone Age or Mesolithic period [6000-3500 B.C.]). The earliest settlement was not in the area covered by the modern-day town centre, however, but two-thirds of a mile to the north on Hambro Hill.

The Mesolithic visitors almost certainly came to the Rayleigh Hills via the River Crouch: several Stone-Age finds have been made on the waterfront at Hullbridge in addition to the ones in Rayleigh.

There is plenty of archaeological evidence for Stone-Age man's presence on Hambro Hill. Many flint implements – including axes, scrapers and arrowheads – have been discovered there and at nearby Drovers Hill (the old name for the incline at the Rayleigh end of the Hockley High Road, on the Rayleigh-Hockley border).

3 Mesolithic flintwork found on Hambro Hill.

It was probably the search for flint nodules for the creation of such tools that first attracted Stone-Age man to the top of the ridge, as there is evidence that many were made there. Later, as the nomadic hunter-gatherers were replaced by settlers who learnt how to farm the land, the value of the site for vantage point and defence reasons ensured its continued occupation.

Apart from the finds at Rayleigh and Hullbridge, Stone-Age implements have also been found some two miles to the south of Hambro Hill in Daws Heath, so the evidence for the inhabitation of this whole area by early man is truly plentiful. It has been speculated that Hambro Hill, with its high vantage point, formed a permanent settlement area for Stone-Age man, with temporary encampments at Hullbridge and Daws Heath.

The area has been fortunate in having several individuals with an active interest in collecting Stone-Age evidence. In the decade before the First World War a local resident, Harry Rand, built up a large collection of flints that he had found in the Hambro Hill area. Much of this collection, with additions contributed by F.N. Hayward, ended up in the then fairly new museum in nearby Southend-on-Sea. A contemporary of Rand, A. Wright, also built up a sizeable local collection which ended up in

4 A tanged and barbed Bronze-Age arrowhead found in the Rayleigh area.

Southend Museum, as did that of another man, T.J. Mays. Finds from all these collections can still be seen on display at the Central Museum in Victoria Avenue, Southend.

BRONZE AGE
After the Stone Age came the Bronze Age and again in Rayleigh it is Hambro Hill that has provided the best evidence of occupation for this period, though finds have also been made at Castle Road and Daws Heath Road.

The principal finds have been of tanged and barbed (i.e. specially shaped) flint arrowheads, several of which are also on display in Southend Central Museum. A flint knife and a bronze spearhead have also been found.

5 Casts of Late Iron-Age urns found on Hambro Hill.

IRON AGE

The Bronze Age was followed by the Iron Age and once again the best evidence for settlement comes from Hambro Hill, showing the importance of the site for continuous human occupation over many centuries.

The most spectacular find was a collection of eight urns, discovered buried in a straight line at the beginning of the 20th century during gravel quarrying operations. Each one contained the cremated remains of a human and it is thought that they may have been a family group burial, possibly originally interred under a mound. A 1910 edition of the *Essex Naturalist* reported that they were initially 'thrown aside as valueless', but fortunately Messrs Rand and Wright salvaged and retained at least two complete pots and some fragments. Some of the pottery later ended up in Colchester Museum, though Southend Museum (not then in existence) has a cast of one of them. There is a school of thought locally that, though the pots were originally classed as Iron-Age, they may actually be early Roman.

Another well-documented case is that of 'three remarkably good specimens of Early Iron Age burial vessels' which, according to the *East Anglian Daily Times* of 12 February

1935, 'caused a stir in antiquarian circles'. They were found in the garden of Mr A.H. Poole and ranged in height from eight inches to two feet. One had ashes inside it; another had evidently been used to store foodstuffs. They were all dated to *c.*500 B.C.

Other urns, bowls and pottery fragments have also been discovered, including some Late Iron-Age finds in The Chase.

ROMANS

The Iron Age came to an abrupt end in A.D. 43, with the invasion of Britain by the Romans. In practice, however, as with all the other periods above, the changeover was not dramatic but gradual.

The south-eastern corner of Essex was not a hugely significant area for the well-travelled and well-organised Romans, being something of a marshland backwater.

In Rayleigh the best Roman find was made in 1850 at White House Farm, the white, weatherboarded 18th-century farmhouse in Eastwood Road, half a mile to the south-east of the modern town centre. According to the 19th-century Rochford historian, Philip Benton, 'a considerable number of Roman denarii contained in a Roman earthen pot were ploughed up by Mark Partner in a field called

Fishponds, upon White House Farm. A Roman copper coin of Hadrian has since been found at the spot and the place examined. Nothing further has been discovered but broken pieces of pottery … The finder sold these coins [to local people] from 4d to one shilling each …'. Benton lists 234 coins sold in this way.

Other small finds of coins and pottery have been made throughout the town and there are also Roman tiles in the walls of Holy Trinity Church (see p.32).

The Roman period ended A.D. *c.*410 when troops were withdrawn to sort out problems at home.

SAXONS

The Romans were succeeded by the Saxons and it was the East Saxons who gave Essex its name.

The Saxons developed the concept of nucleated village centres, which replaced the scattered homesteads and transitional encampments of earlier settlers. They also, after an initial period of comparative disorganisation, created the wider parish structure which supported the villages, establishing a patchwork quilt of communities on the landscape which still survives to this day.

In south-east Essex Saxon settlement is thought to have started in the lower lying plains to the east of the Rayleigh Hills, with the new invaders, like their predecessors, almost certainly coming to the area from the sea and via the rivers. Communities named after people or with descriptive place names, such as Barling ('the people of Baerla') and Prittlewell ('babbling spring'), came first. These were established in easily accessible areas with good farming land, close to water sources and woodland (for fuel, shelter, building materials, etc.) and are thought to have been settled in the late-fifth century and throughout the sixth.

In the hills to the west, where woodland was more extensive and slopes were steeper, it took longer for the Saxons to settle. Essex was once covered in trees, officially known as the 'Wildwood', and surviving areas of ancient woodland around Rayleigh, like Hockley Woods and the Great

6 A Roman coin of Philip I, found in the Rayleigh area.

Wood in Hadleigh, are remnants of this. Villages in the hills to the west of the plain necessarily sprung up in clearings in the woodland.

The name 'Rayleigh' derives from the Saxon words 'raege' and 'leah', meaning 'the clearing of the wild she-goat' (or doe). There are several village names locally ending in 'leah' (Hadleigh, Hockley and Thundersley, for example), all of which sprang up in clearings in woodland. In Rayleigh itself there were the areas of Great and Little Wheatley ('wheat clearing').

These villages in the clearings were not settled until later (Hockley is an exception, as 'Hocca' is a personal name and was therefore slightly earlier), when the more easily accessible places with the most fertile farming land had been exhausted. This probably took place in the seventh century.

Beyond the village- and parish-level of organisation, the Saxons also established the concept of 'Hundreds', administrative districts into which Essex was divided, which were effectively the forerunners of modern local authorities. They were called Hundreds most likely because each district was presided over by 100 men. These men discussed such matters as farming, business and security and enforced the law by acting as a local court. They met in a building in the principal town of the Hundred and meetings were chaired by an individual called the 'Hundred Man' or 'Earldorman'. Each Hundred sent a representative to a county meeting, creating a county-wide body of authority which was effectively the forerunner of the modern-day Essex County Council.

The evolutionary process of parish and Hundred development took place over several

7 A sixth-century Saxon necklace found by Essex County Council's Field Archaeology Unit during excavations in 2002-4 at the former Park School site in Rawreth Lane.

centuries (probably the eighth to 12th centuries for parishes, with the Hundreds in place by some time in the 10th century). When it was complete, Rayleigh village and parish found itself at the extreme western end of a district styled 'Rochford Hundred', which covered the southeast corner of Essex between the Rivers Crouch and Thames and extended from Rawreth, Rayleigh and Hadleigh in the west to Foulness Island in the east. Rochford village, which gave its name to the Hundred, was approximately central geographically, though Rayleigh was for a time the administrative centre.

The Rayleigh Hills effectively marked the boundary between Rochford Hundred and neighbouring Barstable Hundred to the west. Rayleigh, an entirely inland parish, approximately rectangular but with long, narrow protrusions to the north and southwest, was surrounded by eight other parishes (listed clockwise from the north): Hockley; Hawkwell; Rochford; Eastwood; Hadleigh; Thundersley; North Benfleet; and Rawreth. All but Thundersley and North Benfleet were in Rochford Hundred.

Saxons finds have been made throughout the area covered by Rochford Hundred, but until recently the archaeological evidence in Rayleigh was slight, with only silver pennies, a brooch and a stud of any note. However, since the turn of the millennium a Saxon cemetery containing the remains of at least 150 cremation burials has been found beneath the playing fields of the old Park School in Rawreth Lane, which has been demolished to make way for a leisure centre and housing. These burials, each in the form of a ceramic pot containing the burnt remains of the deceased, have been dated to the sixth century from the distinctive, handmade, often highly decorated, pottery vessels that have been used.

Substantial damage was caused to the site by the levelling of the school playing fields in the 1960s, but it nevertheless represents a major find. Various accessories were found amongst the human remains, including knives, buckles, belts and beads. A lack of weapons suggests it was a purely agricultural community. Perhaps the most significant find was in a so-far-unique inhumation burial, where a beautiful 110-bead necklace was discovered.

The layout of Rayleigh High Street also gives a clue to Saxon inhabitation. Linear, with buildings on either side and a church at one end, it is typical of the pattern of a Saxon village.

The Saxons evidently had a significant presence in the locality and Rayleigh as we know it was coming into being.

The next giant step towards the creation of modern Rayleigh would be taken by the Normans.

Two

The Norman Conquest and Rayleigh Castle

The Saxon period of domination came to a sudden end in 1066 with the invasion of England by the Normans, under the leadership of William the Conqueror.

In 1086 William commissioned Domesday Book, a written record of who owned what land, how many people lived or were employed on it, and details of productive resources such as livestock, watermills, woodlands and beehives. Domesday Book recorded the situation in both 1066 and 1086, giving a picture of both late Saxon and early Norman England.

For Rayleigh, this was an important period in the town's history, as it led to the creation of the town as we know it today.

ROBERT FITZWIMARC

The first named individual with a direct connection to Rayleigh is Robert Fitzwimarc (Robert, son of Wimarc).

Robert was landowner, around the time of the Conquest, of what was called 'the Honor of Rayleigh', a collection of estates or manors. In Rayleigh's case this probably included the villages of Hadleigh and Rawreth, neither of which is mentioned in Domesday Book, plus many other lands further afield.

Robert had a complex personal background, being related to both William the Conqueror and Edward the Confessor, King of England from 1042 to 1066. He had met the latter in France sometime before 1042 whilst Edward was in exile and Danish kings were occupying the English throne. When Edward became King he gave Robert substantial landholdings plus the posts of King's Standard Bearer, Constable of England and Sheriff of Essex (amongst others). Robert had responsibility to the King for royal interests in the county, such as landholdings, forests and taxes, and was an important figure in Saxon government.

When Edward died in January 1066 and William the Conqueror defeated Edward's successor, King Harold, at the Battle of Hastings in October, the new King confiscated the landholdings of most of those whom Edward had appointed, removed them from office and replaced them with his own supporters. Robert, however, was one of a small number of Edward's appointees who was allowed to retain his pre-Conquest landholdings and was the only pre-Norman landholder in Essex to do so. This privilege was granted almost certainly because of Robert's own Norman connections and, it has been speculated, possibly even from some sort of involvement in helping William to invade England.

One of William's first acts was to oversee the creation of a network of castles, staffed by loyal Norman noblemen, which could administer law and order over the newly-suppressed Saxon population. What land he did give to individuals was dispersed in comparatively small parcels, reducing the opportunities for landholders to develop extensive heartlands and large gatherings of loyal supporters and build up armies against him.

Robert, who had a wide spread of estates throughout Essex, chose Clavering in the north-west corner of the county as his base. As one of William's trusted supporters, he was allowed to build a castle there. It is possibly the earliest Norman castle in Essex.

8 The Rayleigh skyline before development, showing the town's four major ancient landmarks: the castle (now called 'Rayleigh Mount'), the windmill, Holy Trinity Church and the Dutch Cottage. This photograph is one of several in this book taken by George Dawson and now in the archives of Southend Museums Service. Dawson was excellent at recording information about his photographs. This one was taken at 4.25pm on 12

At the end of a long and illustrious career Robert was buried in Westminster Abbey. He is remembered locally in the name of Fitzwimarc School.

SWEYNE

By the time of Domesday Book in 1086 Robert Fitzwimarc had been succeeded by his son, Sweyne. There are various spellings of his name in circulation. The spelling used here is the one current in Rayleigh. Sweyne is also commemorated in a Rayleigh school name – Sweyne Park.

Sweyne inherited his father's estates and also held the office of Sheriff of Essex. During the next few years he added to his inherited landholdings to become one of the largest landowners in Essex. His lands in the south-eastern corner alone stretched from Rayleigh to Wakering.

Domesday Book gives much information about both Sweyne and Rayleigh, revealing that the town had woodland (described as being enough for 40 pigs), a park and even a vineyard which 'pays 20 measures of wine if it does well'. The population was small, but

land in the manor included areas held by 'four Frenchmen', a sign of the new administration that now held sway.

By far and away Sweyne's greatest legacy for Rayleigh, however, was his castle.

RAYLEIGH CASTLE

The strategic importance of Rayleigh, with its hilltop position and commanding views, had been attracting man since as far back as the Stone Age. Sweyne, who held much land in south-east Essex, must have been familiar with the area, for he chose to move his headquarters from his father's base at Clavering to Rayleigh, where, as Domesday Book records it, 'in this manor Sweyne made his castle'. From here, on a site approximately halfway between the Rivers Thames and Crouch, Sweyne's castle would dominate the countryside and protect his estates, effectively controlling land access to the Rochford Hundred peninsula between the two rivers. Its significance is such that it is the only Essex castle mentioned in Domesday Book.

The site chosen for the castle was a natural promontory on the western side of the Rayleigh

9 Another photograph from the lens of George Dawson, dated the same day as the previous one and taken 15 minutes later. Apart from the High Street area to the right, the centre of Rayleigh was then still largely undeveloped.

Hills, which looked out over the flat land to the west and north. This site was about two-thirds of a mile to the south of the Hambro Hill site which had been chosen by the earliest human visitors, but was in the area where the Saxons had chosen to settle.

An existing natural mound on top of the promontory was increased in height and made more easily defensible by the digging of a ditch on the eastern side and the placing of the dug-out earth on top of the mound, known as a 'motte'. This work was carried out c.1070. The inner edge of the ditch had a ledge at least five feet wide on which there is thought to have been a bank, topped with a wooden palisade for defensive protection.

For the first 70 years or so the castle consisted solely of this raised mound, possibly with some sort of wooden look-out tower on top. However, in the early 12th century the castle's defences were extended by the digging of a ditch around land to the east of the mound, creating a flat, palisaded area for living quarters for the soldiers who manned the castle. This flat area was known as the 'bailey' and with its construction (by c.1140) the castle took on what is recognised as the classic

Norman motte-and-bailey form (a look-out mound with an adjacent palisaded flat area), examples of which can be found throughout Essex and beyond. The modern-day duck pond around one section of the castle occupies the site of the ditch around the motte-and-bailey, though in its original form it was probably never filled with water.

In Rayleigh's case the bailey was actually split into two separately identifiable parts, an inner and outer bailey. The inner bailey was three-quarters of an acre of flat ground where the soldiers, servants, craftsmen and horses lived. It had a defensive ditch around it and a rampart or earth wall running around the top of the slope above the ditch, topped by palisades of wooden stakes, eight inches in diameter and set at intervals of two feet along the crown in a staggered line. The outer bailey covered a further acre to the east, stretching as far as modern-day Bellingham Lane.

In the middle of the 12th century, following a brief period of neglect, the slopes of the motte were reinforced with a covering of Kentish ragstone, a common construction material used in south Essex during this period, usually brought across the Thames by boat. As a result, the motte was increased in height to approximately its current level (50 feet high; altitude over 240 feet). The original ditch between the motte and bailey (technically referred to as the 'fosse') had silted up, so the stones were laid over the top of the silt and a new palisade was built around the side of the motte. The motte's increase in height enabled the castle's defenders to have a better view over both the bailey and the higher ground beyond it to the east. There are records of repairs being made during the reign of Henry II in both 1172-3 and 1183-4, whilst the latter also refers to improvements to 'the King's houses in the castle'.

Further protection was provided in the 12th century by the construction of an additional fortification, the barbican, an earthwork outside the motte-and-bailey area for the defence of the castle entrance. This was positioned on raised ground to the north of the inner bailey, outside the bailey's defensive ditch, built with clay dug from that ditch. It comprised two platforms with timber supports, forming the foundations of a trestle bridge to give access to the castle.

Sometime in the 13th century a deep ditch (fosse) was again cut between the motte and the inner bailey and large stones were mortared together on the rampart on the western end of the inner bailey to raise the height there by up to three feet. On the eastern side of the inner bailey, a cobbled surface was laid onto the rampart, though there was no attempt to raise its height.

As a result of on-going defensive improvements, the eastern rampart of the inner bailey was gradually extended some 40 feet into the bailey's interior. This, and the re-scouring of the fosse to deepen it, would have decreased the available living space within the inner bailey. It is consequently thought likely that buildings and equipment were therefore moved at some stage from the inner bailey to the outer bailey.

ROBERT DE ESSEX
On Sweyne's death (thought to be c.1086), his estates, including Rayleigh Castle, passed to his son Robert FitzSweyne, otherwise known as Robert de Essex.

Unlike his father and grandfather, Robert does not appear to have been a significant figure in the country's government and is thought to have spent a lot of time on his Rayleigh estate. He was certainly familiar with south-east Essex as in c.1110 he founded the religious house of Prittlewell Priory, some five miles to the south-east of Rayleigh, where he, and before him his father, was lord of the manor.

HENRY DE ESSEX
Robert died in 1135 and his estates passed to his son, Henry de Essex. Like his forefathers, Henry held the post of King's Standard Bearer and 'was a man of high renown among the first in the realm', but unlike them he was unfortunately destined for disgrace.

According to contemporary sources, Henry was accompanying King Henry II on a campaign in Wales in 1157 when the English were attacked. In the midst of the battle he threw down the standard and declared that the King had been killed, causing the English to panic and flee. Other noblemen rallied round, however, and it soon became clear that the King was alive and well.

Henry's reputation was tarnished by this event, but he remained in favour for several more years until a personal feud with Robert de Montfort brought memory of his actions to the fore. Robert accused Henry of cowardice in Wales and challenged him to a duel. Henry lost and ended his days in a monastery in Reading. His estates, including the Honor of Rayleigh, were forfeited to the Crown. The de Essex family's period of supremacy had come to a surprisingly ignominious end.

Nevertheless, where Rayleigh Castle was concerned, Henry was successful. He commissioned much of the extension work referred to above, including creating the bailey, facing the motte with ragstone and increasing its height.

HUBERT DE BURGH
By the turn of the 13th century, King John had acceded to the throne. In a troubled reign, he had to face uprisings from various Norman

barons and baronial-inspired invasions from France. One of his greatest allies in these difficult times was to be the next significant figure in Rayleigh's castle ownership – Hubert de Burgh.

De Burgh was born in Norfolk *c.*1175 and probably saw service as a boy to John's immediate predecessor and brother, Richard I. He was John's chamberlain by 1198 and in June 1215 was made justiciar, the chief judicial officer of the realm. He supported the King both politically and on the battlefield. His military exploits included a superb defence of Dover Castle against the French King's son, Prince Louis (with English baronial backing), in 1216 and a second successful defence the following year. He also defeated a French invasionary force of 80 ships in 1217 in England's first large-scale naval victory, the Battle of Sandwich.

The death of King John in 1216 brought about a compromise peace between the Crown and the barons, and John's successor, the young Henry III, was looked after by the regent, William Marshall. When Marshall died in 1219, de Burgh became the dominant figure in government.

Amongst the innumerable possessions given to Hubert by John and Henry in reward for his services were the Manor of Rayleigh and the neighbouring Manor of Hadleigh.

Unlike his de Essex predecessors, however, de Burgh did not want Rayleigh as his headquarters, preferring the Thameside location of his Hadleigh manor, which offered a better chance of spotting and repelling any French invasions than did the existing inland stronghold at Rayleigh. In about 1230 he received a licence to build a new castle at Hadleigh and the 160-year-old castle at Rayleigh began for the first time to lose some of its importance. Nevertheless, some further work was carried out at Rayleigh Castle during the late 12th and 13th centuries (as outlined above) and it could be that de Burgh was responsible for some of this work.

Hubert's dominance in government and favouritism with the King made him many enemies. The barons were agitating

10 The only known picture of Hubert de Burgh, 13th-century owner of Rayleigh Castle. De Burgh preferred the Thameside location of Hadleigh as a local headquarters and built the castle there as a replacement for the one at Rayleigh. He may have used some of the materials from Rayleigh Castle to build the Hadleigh one.

for concessions, and several failed military expeditions in Wales and the continuing loss of English-held lands in France contributed to their growing unrest. As the young King reached maturity he began to hanker after reclaiming lands in France that had been lost by his father, and the barons began to poison his mind with ideas about the alleged treachery of de Burgh.

In 1232, on largely trumped-up charges, Hubert was arrested and dismissed from office. He spent two years detained in Merton Priory and Devizes Castle during several trials and retrials and at one stage was dragged (against the traditional rules of refuge) from the sanctuary at Brentwood chapel and taken to the Tower of London.

After a period of imprisonment, he was eventually released and pardoned. He was reconciled with the King to a degree, but never regained the power or authority that he had once wielded. He died in 1243 at Banstead in Surrey.

Hubert's castle at Rayleigh passed on his death to his third wife Margaret (d.1259) and then to his son (by his first marriage) John. It was returned to the Crown either after John's death or, according to some sources, towards the end of his life in order to clear his debts.

SUBSEQUENT OWNERS AND DECLINE

Henry III's successor, Edward I, gave Rayleigh to his Queen, Eleanor of Castile. She established a horse-breeding centre at the castle which continued after her death in 1290. The King himself evidently planned to visit the castle at some stage for in 1282 money was requested for repairs 'in the King's great chamber against the King's arrival'. In 1301 the Prior of nearby Prittlewell Priory was commissioned to repair a house of the King's at Rayleigh.

This was, however, the last period in which the castle had any importance, as after this it seems to have fallen into disuse. This is not surprising. With the decline of baronial disputes within England and the country now more concerned about possible attack from abroad, the Thamesside castle at Hadleigh became more important than the inland one at Rayleigh. From 1277 to 1303 there are several documentary references to the castle being used merely for pasture.

In the early 1360s Queen Philippa, wife of Edward III, gave instructions for a 'chamber' of some 40 feet by 18 feet to be removed from the site. This must have been a wooden building, for there is no evidence of any stone structures there. At the same time, Edward was carrying out a large-scale rebuilding and improvement of Hadleigh Castle – a clear sign to anyone in any doubt where the priorities for defence now lay.

In 1394 the death knell for Rayleigh Castle was finally sounded when Richard II gave permission for his tenants at Rayleigh to quarry for stones in 'the foundations of a certain old castle which used to be in that town'. After over 300 years, the usefulness of Rayleigh Castle as a defensive stronghold had come to an end.

LATER HISTORY

From the late 14th to the late 17th centuries Rayleigh's castle seems largely to have been forgotten.

In 1631 it was described as 'a ruined castle', a slightly misleading description for an earthwork fortification. Towards the end of that century the inner bailey site was occupied by farm buildings and from then until the 1920s much of the old castle site was grazed with sheep. Nevertheless, the location of the earthworks was evidently well-known. By 1768 the Essex historian, Philip Morant, was describing it as 'a famous piece of antiquity' which 'yields an agreeable prospect all over the [surrounding] country[side]'.

In Morant's day the castle was owned by Chester Moore Hall, inventor of the achromatic lens system for the telescope, who is commemorated in the parish church of Sutton (near Rochford). Rochford Hundred historian Philip Benton confirms that it subsequently passed through the Hall family until being acquired by the Neave family. It was in the hands of the trustees of the young Sir Thomas Neave, 5th Baronet of Dagnam Park at Noak Hill near Romford, in the 1880s when Benton was writing.

A famous photograph from 1909 shows the castle site lightly covered in trees and bushes, but the subsequent growth in the surrounding town and the consequent reduction in agriculture

11 A close-up of Rayleigh Mount, *c*.1908, showing the now sailless windmill and the tower of Holy Trinity Church. This view is now obscured by trees.

and grazing have allowed the undergrowth to grow unchecked. This growth has continued until the present day and it is now quite difficult to make out some of the original castle features.

E.B. FRANCIS

Modern-day interest in Rayleigh Castle was sparked by a local antiquarian, Edward Belcham Francis (1850-1939), a retired Indian civil servant and amateur archaeologist, who purchased the castle in 1909 to prevent its loss to development and carried out some excavations at the site. Francis lived in Rayleigh High Street (in the building now occupied by Lloyds Bank) and his garden backed onto the castle site.

When Francis acquired it, very little was known about the castle. Some antiquarians thought that it was a Stone-Age or Iron-Age earthwork. Its modern-day name, 'Rayleigh Mount', survives as a reminder of this confusion.

In 1840 a shaft was sunk into the top of the motte but nothing was found. Francis' approach was much more scientific, with research through historical documents backing up a two-year programme of archaeological investigations on the site. He usually worked alone, or sometimes with one or two assistants, and shared his findings with other well-known Essex local historians, including Miller Christy and Colchester Museum's A.G. Wright, both of

12 The Essex Union Hounds in Rayleigh High Street, showing in the background the *Crown Hotel* and Edward Francis' house (now Lloyds Bank). Francis was the first to show an active interest in the history of Rayleigh Castle and carried out the first significant archaeological excavations there.

whom visited the site. Towards the end of his initial period of research he documented all his findings in a paper which he read out at a meeting of the Essex Archaeological Society, held in Rayleigh on 10 September 1910.

'Since becoming possessed of the site of the castle in Rayleigh in July 1909,' Francis began, 'I've taken much interest in its history, have caused considerable research to be made among the ancient documents preserved at the Public Record Office and carried on, by means of the

13 A Norman coin from the reign of King Stephen (*c.*1140), which was found during excavations at Rayleigh Castle.

spade, extensive explorations upon its site.'

His research in the field revealed previously unknown foundations (though most were later dated to the 17th century), whilst his research in historical documents revealed much of the information and many of the dates referred to above. As well as the masonry foundations, he found timber gateposts, pottery, bones, oyster shells, charcoal, bronze statues, brooches and padlocks, iron padlocks, crossbow bolts and arrowheads, seven silver pennies from the reign of King Stephen and a considerable number of Roman tiles, the latter presumed to have been used as 'hardcore' by the Norman builders.

Francis was not a professional archaeologist, but he had a boundless enthusiasm which comes across in his papers and it is to him that we owe much of our knowledge of the history of Rayleigh Castle.

Like his predecessors, Robert Fitzwimarc and Sweyne, he is remembered locally in the name of one of Rayleigh's schools.

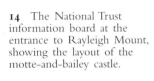

14 The National Trust information board at the entrance to Rayleigh Mount, showing the layout of the motte-and-bailey castle.

NATIONAL TRUST OWNERSHIP

In 1923 Francis gave the castle to the National Trust, on whose Local Committee he served until 1935. It is still managed and maintained by the local National Trust group, with the assistance of Rochford District and Rayleigh Town Councils.

In 1959 the Rayleigh Mount Local Committee of the National Trust commissioned Leonard Helliwell and D.G. McLeod to carry out extensive excavations on the site, which they did during the three years 1959-61. Their work built on that of Francis, showing that there had been six clear phases of development. They discovered two hearths in the centre of the bailey, one with an accumulation of ashes, bones and pot sherds swept away to its edges, which indicated a lengthy period of regular use. They also found traces of timber-framed structures in the north-west corner of the bailey, the oldest dating from the late 13th century. These included a large, chalk-floored building and a smithy, the latter identified from pits in the clay found to contain iron fragments and slag. Archaeological finds included arrowheads, horseshoes, pottery, various iron implements (e.g. keys), a coin from the reign of King Stephen, animal bones and 17th-century clay pipes.

In 1969-70 Mr McLeod returned to supervise further excavations under the sponsorship of the Ministry of Public Buildings & Works. These were concentrated in the barbican area and resulted in the discovery of the timber trestle bridge and related defences mentioned above.

In 1983 and 1985 excavations in the outer bailey were carried out by Essex County Council's Archaeology Section on the site of the demolished *Regal* cinema. These located part of the outer bailey ditch, dating it to *c*.12th century. A similar ditch was also seen in the foundation trenches of an extension at 23 Bellingham Lane in 1997. The scarp of the outer bailey ditch, which drops down into the gardens of the houses that now back onto it, seems to have been used to mark the boundary between it and the houses since at least the 15th or 16th century.

Further excavations were carried out in the outer bailey in 1997. Several archaeological deposits were found, dating from the tenth to the 13th centuries.

The public have access free-of-charge seven days a week to all parts of Rayleigh Castle except the barbican, though many of the historical features are difficult to determine underneath the extensive tree cover (the

15   An aerial photograph of Rayleigh Mount showing increased tree cover since the days of George Dawson and the importance of the site today as a wildlife and recreational area in the centre of the built-up town. Bellingham Lane is in the right foreground, with London Hill extending behind the windmill towards the railway line.

National Trust now runs it principally as a haven for wildlife, rather than as a heritage site). From the top of the motte, through the trees, one can glimpse the surrounding countryside to the north-west, showing what an important vantage point this was when the castle was active.

The castle now provides an important wildlife habitat in the centre of Rayleigh, with over 30 species of tree and 160 species of herbaceous plants. Butterflies, birds, squirrels, bats and wildflowers are amongst the many natural attractions. It is also a valuable educational resource for local schoolchildren.

There is no doubting the significance of the castle in the history of Rayleigh town. Its presence caused a settlement to grow up around it and the Essex historian Norman Scarfe has described it, justifiably, as 'the motte-and-bailey castle that brought a town into being'.

Three

Rayleigh Park and the Ancient Woodland

The Domesday Book entry for Rayleigh mentions a 'park'. But where was this park? And what did it look like?

Norman parks were large areas of meadow and woodland, covering hundreds of acres. Their boundaries were defined by law and they were generally in the ownership of the King. They were used for hunting (mostly for deer) and as a source of raw materials such as timber.

With its proximity to London, Essex was a popular place for park creation and in its south-east corner there were four parks: Hadleigh, Thundersley, Rayleigh/Eastwood and Rochford.

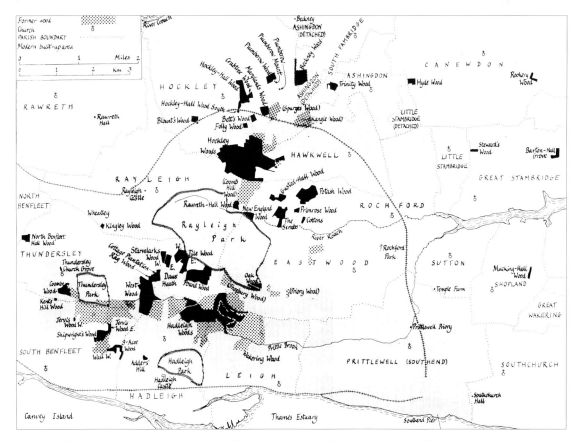

16 A sketch map of the woods and parkland of south-east Essex, showing the location of Rayleigh Park, overlaid onto a map of the historic parishes of the area. This map was produced by the well-known woodland historian, Oliver Rackham.

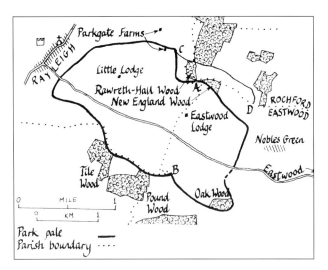

17 Another sketch by Oliver Rackham, showing a close-up of Rayleigh Park, complete with Rayleigh (Little) and Eastwood Lodges, the Eastwood/Rayleigh Road, Fisher's & Stevens' Farms, local woodland and parish boundaries.

RAYLEIGH PARK

Much research into the history and location of Rayleigh Park has been carried out by the landscape and woodland historian, Oliver Rackham, who has conjectured that probably about one-fifth of Essex was covered in woodland at the time of the Norman Conquest.

It is clear from Domesday Book that a park was in existence in 1086, but no indication is given as to its size or boundaries. Early records are scarce and it is not until about 1250 that improved records of land management shed some light on this. Mr Rackham has pieced these together to come up with a composite picture of what the Park might have looked like.

Rayleigh Park lay to the east of the village centre, extending at least as far into neighbouring Eastwood parish as modern-day Progress Road and straddling the main route between the two settlements – Eastwood Road, Rayleigh and Rayleigh Road, Eastwood. Oak Wood on the A127, near the top end of Progress Road, is thought to have marked the furthest south-eastern corner of the park, with the furthest north-eastern corner being somewhere in the vicinity of Flemings Farm at Nobles Green. The

south-western corner followed approximately the line of Dawes Heath Road from the A127 to Eastwood Road, whilst the north-western corner followed approximately the line of Bull Lane. Much of the southern boundary of the Rayleigh part of the park was also the southern boundary of the wider Rayleigh parish.

The park covered a mixed terrain from the slopes on the eastern side of the Rayleigh Hills to lower, flatter land further east along the Rayleigh Road. Early parks rarely crossed parish boundaries, so it could be that the Eastwood portion was added later as an extension. The name 'Eastwood' comes from that settlement's geographical position east of the woodland (and parkland) of Rayleigh.

In the late 12th century Rayleigh Park was in the ownership of King Henry II. Henry's son, King John, was a regular visitor to nearby Thundersley Park and it seems likely that he would have visited Rayleigh Park, too.

Throughout the 13th century there are many references in official documents to the south-east Essex parks. In 1214 timber felled in Rayleigh Park was ordered to be transported to the River Thames for shipment to Dover Castle. In 1233 12 oaks from the park were sent to the Bishop of Winchester for the making of planks. The following year five trees unsuitable for timber production were given to the King's chaplain for firewood. In 1235 two bucks and six does were given freely to Ralf Bernardson to enable him to stock a park of his own.

In 1322 the parson of Eastwood church successfully claimed a tithe of the foals coming from the stud which had been operating in Rayleigh Park for as long as anyone could remember. This could have been connected with the horse-breeding activities instituted by Queen Eleanor (see p.12).

In 1361, another Eastwood parson was allowed to make an alteration to long-standing rights to pasture pigs in the Park and replace them with an increased number of cattle. Also during the 1360s birch underwood from the Park was sold to help finance Edward III's large-scale rebuilding of Hadleigh Castle (see p.12).

18   Some of the old boundaries from the now lost Rayleigh Park still survive. This woodbank, marking the Park (and parish) boundary, can still be seen in the north-eastern corner of Pound Wood. (See also illustration 17 opposite.)

In 1380 Geoffrey Dersham and Thomas Ocle (the latter being yet another Eastwood parson) were appointed 'to cut down and sell … a suitable amount of underwood in the King's parks and woods of Hadleigh, Rayleigh and Thundersley … and with the money obtained to pay the costs of enclosing the coppices thereby made, delivering the residue to John Blake, clerk of works, for repair of [Hadleigh] castle'.

King Edward I visited Rayleigh Park at least three times between 1272 and 1307. By this stage, timber production and pasture were the most important uses. Substantial income was derived from the latter in the year 1331-2. Hunting, common elsewhere, is thought to have been minimal in the south-east Essex parks.

The last monarch to show any real interest in Rayleigh Park was Henry VIII (reigned 1509-47). The Rochford Hundred historian, Philip Benton, records that in 1530 deer from Rayleigh were used to replenish the stock at Greenwich Park.

By this stage, however, the park was coming to the end of its useful life. In 1544 it was 'disparked', i.e. officially removed from royal park status and accompanying restrictions, and was sold. It consisted then mainly of grassland, with a number of large ancient trees dotted around. It was perhaps as much as 1000 acres in size.

The park survived only another 40 years, being destroyed on the death of its owner, Edward Bury, in 1583.

Almost the whole of the perimeter of the park survived into the 19th century as field boundaries. Even today it is possible to trace sections of it. In the south, the curving eastern boundary of Oak Wood in Eastwood (which was inside the park) and parts of the

19 The *Rayleigh Lodge* public house and restaurant, on the site of one of the two original lodges of Rayleigh Park.

20 Eastwood Lodge, pictured in late spring 2003, when the adjacent site was being developed for housing.

northern boundaries of Pound and Tile Woods in Thundersley (which were outside) still follow the line of the park perimeter. In the north, the southern boundary of New England Wood (which was outside the park) is still also true to the original perimeter line.

PARK LODGES

Most Royal Parks had park lodges – buildings which served as a meeting point and administration centre for the park. Rayleigh was no exception.

In this case, as the park straddled the boundary between two parishes, there were two lodges, one in each parish, and the last lodge buildings both survive.

Rayleigh Lodge stands in what is now The Chase (a classic park term). It has been used as both a farmhouse and a hotel, but is now the *Rayleigh Lodge* public house. It dates from the 16th century and is claimed to have been built by Henry VIII to provide a discreet meeting place for him and Anne Boleyn, whose family lived in nearby Rochford (*c*.1530s). The park's last owner, Edward Bury, is also believed to have lived there. Over the years, the building has been much altered and extended.

It is possible that the 'chamber' moved to Rayleigh Park from Rayleigh Castle by Queen Philippa *c*.1362-3 (see p.12) was a predecessor of the current building.

In the 1830s and early 1840s Rayleigh Lodge was home to Edward Mee. In 1872 it was known as Lodge Farm. In 1925, when it was again called Rayleigh Lodge, it was occupied by C.A. Cecil.

Eastwood Lodge stands hard up against the Rayleigh-Eastwood boundary in what is now Rayleigh Avenue. Like Rayleigh Lodge, it dates from at least the early 16th century, with subsequent alterations.

In 1925 it was occupied by J. Foreman, but for most of the 20th century it was owned by the Field Lane Foundation, which used it as a residential and nursing home. Field Lane acquired the property in 1936 as a holiday home for young children, but it was requisitioned by the military during the Second World War and was not used again until 1946. In that year, it was converted for use as a holiday home for older people.

By the late 1950s, as the Foundation began to cater increasingly for less able-bodied elderly individuals, the holiday use was abandoned and the home was adapted to provide accommodation for 42 residents who needed nursing care. The building was extended to cater for this use, the extension being officially opened by the Marquis of Aberdeen on 27 July 1957. A further extension was opened in 1963. The building closed in 1999 when the costs of maintaining it became too onerous.

In 2002 it was sold for development and, although the lodge building is being retained, the land around it is being developed for housing.

KINGLEY WOOD

One other area of ancient woodland that deserves a mention at this stage is Kingley Wood. This has no connection whatsoever with Rayleigh Park, but is of a similar period to some of the woods mentioned above that abutted the park's perimeter. In fact, it is the only truly ancient wood, i.e. the only survivor of the original wildwood, in Rayleigh, though many others (including the extensive Hockley Woods in the north) abut the parish boundary.

Kingley Wood is situated to the south-west of Rayleigh town centre, adjacent to the A127 to the west of Rayleigh Weir, and is accessible from the bottom end of Western Road, via Great Wheatley Road. The A127 at this point goes through a curved, two-level cutting through the Rayleigh Hills which will be very familiar to local motorists, but much of the woodland that is visible from the road is actually secondary woodland which has grown up alongside the original, older wood behind it. This older wood extends northwards away from the road along the hillside on the western edge of the Hills. The slope of the wood is quite steep and over the years there have been several landslips inside it.

Kingley Wood takes its name from its one-time Crown ownership. In 1621 it was referred to as the 'King's Wood'. In the 19th century it was recorded as 'King's Hill Wood' and 'Kingsley Wood'. Before the A127 was constructed, it was accessed via what is now called Kingsley Lane (actually in Thundersley parish).

The wood is very rich in its diversity of flora – one of the richest for its size in the whole of eastern England. Benton wrote that 'the wood is a very pretty one, full of undergrowth; the wood anemone and hyacinth abound, and picnics are sometimes held there'. A hundred years later Oliver Rackham counted 77 plant species in the wood's 3.4 acres. Of special note are bluebells, a classic indicator of

21   Kingley Wood and information board.

ancient woodland, plus rowan, hawkweed, hops and cow-wheat. Tree cover is predominantly hornbeam and oak. Unfortunately, the southern part of the original wood was lost to road-cutting when the A127 was dualled in the late 1930s and there has been some encroachment on the north from housing but, as mentioned above, new woodland has sprung up along the sides of the road cutting so there has been a net increase in woodland though it is not yet as rich as the original ancient woodland which was lost.

Historically, the wood is thought to have been home to one of the most bizarre ceremonies of south-east Essex, the so-called Lawless or Whispering Court (more commonly associated with Rochford, to which it was later transferred). The business of the 'court' was ostensibly to record the tenure of, and collect rents from, several local farms. Attendees met annually by starlight 'upon the first cock-crowing' (a lawless hour) and proceedings were carried out in whispers and written down with a piece of charcoal.

Exactly when this procedure started is unclear, but it could date back to at least the 13th century. It is thought to have been established as a punishment to those attending for their involvement in conspiring against a usually absent Lord of the Manor, who was unexpectedly resident in the district one night and overheard conspiratorial whispers among his tenants outside his home when being awoken at midnight by a cockerel. Benton thought that 'this spot upon a dark and rainy night, surrounded by the roughs of the District, must have given the homagers attending, the blues, which the fumes of punch imbibed could hardly dissipate'.

Philip Morant, another Essex historian, described the court as 'a whimsical custom … of which the origin is unknown … The time is the Wednesday morning next after Michaelmas Day upon the first cock crowing, without any kind of light but such as the heavens will afford … they are all to whisper to each other … and he that owes suit and service thereto and appears not, forfeits to the Lord double his rent every hour he is absent …'.

Morant was writing about the court when it was in Rochford, but John Weever, author of a 1631 book on 'funeral monuments', referred to it under Rayleigh when travelling between the two towns. Benton was in no doubt that the court had originated in Kingley Wood, the hillside of which would have made a good natural amphitheatre, asserting that:

> There has been considerable doubt expressed by the incredulous and even by the learned in these latter days as to the Lawless Court having ever been held at Rayleigh, but we shall produce such a mass of evidence as to the site of the original King's Hill having been in this parish, as to silence all future criticism.

He did what he promised, compiling a definitive account from various sources showing that the court was meeting in Rayleigh before 1631 but was transferred to Rochford later in the 17th century. He thought that the confusion might have arisen because the court was often referred to as being in Rochford Hundred and the ill-informed might have taken this to mean Rochford town.

The building where the court was held in Rochford was named 'King's Hill' after the original Rayleigh location. It still stands, in East Street, complete with a five-feet high 'whispering post' (dated 1867), around which the court met, in the grounds.

In Benton's day (1880s) there were at least 14 properties paying rent at the Lawless Court, ranging from Down Hall in Rayleigh in the west of the Hundred to property in North Shoebury in the east. During his research, Benton discovered two volumes of the records of the Honor of Rayleigh 'lately doing service as footstools in a lawyer's office'!

A contemporary of Benton, Henry William King, another well-known antiquarian, was also convinced that the Lawless Court was originally held at Rayleigh. At a meeting of the Essex Archaeological Society in Rochford on 26 May 1891 he read a lengthy paper summarising his own findings and deconstructing, line by line, the claims of a colleague that it had only ever been held in Rochford.

By the late 19th century the original purpose of the court had become secondary to entertainment and revelry. Young men (in particular) would rampage through the town (Rochford), carrying flaming torches and crowing like cockerels until the early hours. As this got increasingly out of hand, the court's days became numbered and it was finally closed down in 1892.

Kingley Wood is also referred to as 'Shrieking Boy Wood' (not the only wood to carry that designation), a name said to have been derived from the murder of a boy nearby by a farm labourer in the 19th century.

Kingley Wood is open to the public at all reasonable times.

Four

The Fragmentation of the Honor of Rayleigh and the Emergence of the Rayleigh Manors

❖

The Honor of Rayleigh was an administrative area which spanned several parishes and, within those parishes, incorporated several manors. Over time, the lands comprising the Honor were granted by the King to different individuals and the whole Honor duly became fragmented into its constituent parts.

In Rayleigh parish, within the Honor, there was originally just one manor. This was known, not surprisingly, as Rayleigh Manor, with its headquarters being Rayleigh Castle. Eventually, this too became sub-divided until there were four separate manors in total.

It seems likely that this process of fragmentation began with the return to the Crown of ownership of the Honor during the life or after the death of John de Burgh in the latter half of the 13th century (see p.12). The whole Honor and its constituent parts had hitherto been kept intact. Hubert de Burgh and, before him, the Fitzwimarc/de Essex family had been granted everything. These grants were sometimes made in groups of smaller parcels, such as when Hubert de Burgh was granted the Manor of Rayleigh and the Manor of Hadleigh, but they were smaller parcels that still made up a whole. However, times were changing, and increasingly smaller grants to a wider number of individuals were becoming more common. More people had power and influence, too, and the money to purchase landholdings where the opportunity arose.

However this process began, the importance of the Honor began to decline and the respective importance of its constituent parts began to increase.

RAYLEIGH MANOR

Rayleigh Manor itself remained in Crown ownership until 1340, when it was given to William de Bohun, whose family were major Essex landowners throughout the 13th and 14th centuries. On William's death it was inherited by his son Humphrey, Earl of Essex, but Humphrey died young in the early 1370s without a male heir and the estate was again returned to the Crown.

In 1380 King Richard II granted the manor to Aubrey de Vere, 10th Earl of Oxford. The de Veres had an even greater Essex pedigree than the de Bohuns, flourishing in the county from the 11th to early 18th centuries. Their base was in the north of the county at Castle Hedingham, but they did have an earlier connection with Rayleigh as Robert de Essex (see p.10) had married Alice de Vere.

Aubrey de Vere died in 1400 and by a restriction on the subsequent inheritance of the manor it passed to the family of Edmund, Duke of York, fifth son of King Edward III. Edmund died in 1402 and the manor passed to his son Edward, who was killed at the Battle of Agincourt in 1415. Some of Edward's possessions remained in the ownership of his wife, Philippa, until she died in 1431 and, after that, the ownership of Rayleigh Manor was once again returned to the Crown.

There it remained until the 1530s when King Henry VIII granted it jointly to Thomas Boleyn, father of Anne and himself Earl of Ormonde and Wiltshire, and his son George Boleyn (Anne's brother), Viscount Rochford. The family had local connections, living at

22 Richard, Lord Rich, lord of the manor of Rayleigh during the 16th century.

nearby Rochford Hall. Their ownership of Rayleigh Manor was brief, however, with George and Anne both being beheaded in 1536, having fallen out of favour with Henry, and their father dying only three years later.

Ownership of many of the Boleyns' local estates passed through Anne's sister Mary to the latter's son, Henry Carey, who later became Lord Hunsdon. In 1553 Carey sold the manor to a leading figure in 16th-century politics, Richard, Lord Rich, a shrewd lawyer who frequently changed allegiances to suit his own ends. Rich employed a deliberate strategy of acquiring extensive landholdings throughout Essex, with seats at Leez Priory (near Great Leighs) and Rochford Hall.

It seems likely that the ownership of Rayleigh Manor was subsequently lost to the Rich family for a period (perhaps due to some political machinations) and it is possible that it returned at some stage to the family of Henry

Carey. By the 1620s it was in the ownership of the Rich family again, being held by Robert Rich, 2nd Earl of Warwick, great-grandson of Richard. It is thought to have been Robert who moved the Lawless Court to Rochford (see pp.21-2), as it would have been much more conveniently placed for him here with his seat at Rochford Hall.

Robert Rich died in 1658 and the manor passed through the Warwick line to one of six co-heirs, Daniel, Earl of Nottingham, who acquired it in 1678. Daniel sold the manor and advowson of the church (the right of appointing the incumbent, originally divested in the monks of Prittlewell Priory) to Robert Bristow, in whose family it remained until the 1860s.

The Rochford Hundred historian, Philip Benton, traced the ancestry of the Bristow family back to the late 13th century. Many family members held important positions under Henry IV, Henry VIII, Edward VI, Mary, Elizabeth I and James I. They also held many estates in Essex at different times.

Robert Bristow and his son and grandson (both also called Robert) all served as MP for Winchelsea. The second Robert married Sarah Ward, daughter of Sir John Ward, Alderman of London, and Lord Mayor in 1719.

In 1869, with no male heir surviving beyond infancy, the Bristows sold the manor to Alfred Wyatt Digby, a solicitor.

The last recorded Lord of the Manor of Rayleigh is James Rogers, who sold the rights to Rayleigh Parish Council in the 1890s.

WHEATLEY MANOR
To the south-west of Rayleigh Manor was the Manor of Wheatley (also spelt 'Whatl(e)y'). This must formerly have been important in its own right, since it is mentioned by name separately from Rayleigh in Domesday Book.

Wheatley, too, belonged to John de Burgh, but was granted by him to Sir John Hardel(l), who subsequently gave it as a wedding gift, with his daughter Alice, to William FitzWarin, then gentleman of the bedchamber to King Edward I.

23 Great Wheatley Farm, still rural and secluded, has survived the extensive development which has befallen other parts of the town.

The manor then descended by inheritance to Robert Knivet, second son of Sir John Knivet, Lord Chancellor. The property remained in the Knivet family until the early 16th century, when it passed by marriage to the Clopton family. It was subsequently sold several times until 1718, when it was bought by Sir William Humphreys, Lord Mayor of London in 1715.

By 1768 the manor had been divided into two, as Great and Little Wheatley. In 1840 both properties were in the ownership of an absentee landowner, Major John Fane. Great Wheatley was occupied by Thomas and Charles Hurrell. Little Wheatley was occupied by Litchfield Moseley. In the 1880s both properties were still in Fane's ownership,

24 Great Wheatley Road, *c*.1913. Great Wheatley Farm, on the site of one of the original Rayleigh manors, still exists at the end of this road.

25 New woodland and housing on the former lands of Little Wheatley Manor.

though the manor was by then described as 'extinct'.

The manor house of Great Wheatley survives, in a secluded location at the end of Great Wheatley Road. It dates from at least the 16th century, with later additions. In 1903 a Mr Waller was tenant of Great Wheatley Farm, but the best-remembered 20th-century owner was Norman Kingston, who died in late December 2002 at the age of 88. Mr Kingston, who grew up in Rayleigh and was a farmer in the town for most of his life, was also active in the Rayleigh Rotary Club and at the town's United Reformed Church.

The manor house of Little Wheatley, which dated from the 17th century, stood at the end of Little Wheatley Chase. A housing estate now stands on the site, but 64 acres of the surrounding land was planted by the Woodland Trust in the 1990s as 'Wheatley Wood'.

DOWN HALL MANOR

The Manor of Down Hall lay to the north of the village centre. The manor house stood to the east of Down Hall Road, approximately where Down Hall Close is now. It is not clear how or when this manor came into being, though it is thought likely that it was created by John de Burgh. Alternatively, it could have been created by the King or by William de Bohun.

26 Down Hall from a sales brochure in 1923, when it was described as a 'valuable freehold old-world country residence'.

27 Down Hall Road, which led to the manors of Down Hall and Harbutts/Harberges, pictured *c*.1915.

The recognised Essex place-names expert, Dr P.H. Reaney, says that it was the home of one John de la Dune in 1248 and was recorded as Down(e)hall(e) in 1375.

Like Wheatley Manor, Down Hall descended by inheritance into the ownership of Robert Knivet and, through the Knivet family, to the Cloptons. In 1719, it too was purchased by Sir William Humphreys, this time from a Mr Downes, a London attorney.

By the end of the century it was in the ownership of Thomas Slye and his wife Mary. When the latter died in 1808 she left it to her nephew, Thomas Brewitt of Wickford. The Brewitts had a large presence in south-east Essex at this time, with family branches at Wickford, Downham and South Benfleet.

Thomas retained ownership of the property until his death in 1830, when it passed to his son, also Thomas (died 1857). Thomas junior was very active in local affairs, serving as churchwarden for many years from the 1820s to the 1850s. In January 1830 he chaired

an important rates meeting of Rayleigh parishioners.

Thomas senior was interred in the family vault at Downham, but Thomas junior and his first wife Sophia were buried at Rayleigh.

Thomas junior's daughter, Mary, married already-twice-married Dr George Hilliard and the manor descended to their son, Thomas Edward Brewitt Hilliard, who chose to live in London. Mary died in Romford in 1870 but is buried with her parents at Holy Trinity Church in Rayleigh and the font there is also dedicated to her.

By 1875 Down Hall was in the occupancy of Thomas William Offin, a descendant of the Offin family of Hutton.

A field at the junction of Down Hall Road and London Road (in the vicinity of the *Traveller's Joy* pub) was once home to a gallows and the name 'Gallows Field' existed into the early 20th century. This was a prominent road junction on the way into the village from London and the execution of criminals here would have sent a clear message to any outsiders intending to commit crimes in the village.

Philip Benton was told by an elderly local resident, Thomas Linggood, that the stumps of the gallows had been unearthed 'within living memory' (early 19th century). The Linggoods were an old Rayleigh family, trading principally as blacksmiths.

HARBERGES, HARBERTS OR HARBUTTS MANOR

The Manor of Harberges (known in its later days as Harberts or Harbutts) also lay to the north of the village centre, with the manor house also in what is now Down Hall Road, approximately in the vicinity of Lakeside and Eastcheap. It took its name from one-time owners the Harberge or Haverburgh family, who originated from Market Harborough in Leicestershire.

The Haverburgh family held property in Rayleigh c.1293-1363 and probably longer. Helen Hardell, another daughter of Sir John (see above), was married to Sir William de Hareburgh, a corruption of Haverburgh.

In 1422 the manor was owned by John Baud, whose son William inherited it upon John's death in that year.

Sometime in the late 15th or early 16th century additional lands in neighbouring Rawreth and Hockley parishes were annexed to the manor, greatly increasing its acreage. Thomas Lawrence held this increased landholding in 1551, but by 1576 it was in the occupation of John Wincoll, who held it on behalf of Lord Hunsdon.

Thomas White held it in 1623, but by 1719, like Wheatley and Down Hall, it was in the ownership of Sir William Humphreys. This meant that all three new manors which had been created out of the original single Rayleigh Manor some 400 years or so earlier were united again as one.

The property was advertised for auction in 1791 and by the early 19th century it was in the ownership of the Neave family. The Neaves sold it to Thomas Brewitt junior of Down Hall (see above) c.1835. Brewitt left it to his grandson, Thomas Edward Brewitt Hilliard.

By the 1880s the manors of Down Hall and Harberges, both in the ownership of the Brewitt/Hilliard family, had been merged and the manor of Harberges had been made officially 'extinct'.

Five

The Early Development of Rayleigh Village

By the time of the destruction of Rayleigh Park in the late 16th century, Rayleigh village had developed into an important local centre. The Norman castle and the administrative area of which it was the focus had encouraged the growth of the original Saxon settlement. The castle and the park, with their respective successive owners' prominent positions in the kingdom, had both brought fame and prosperity to the area. As a result, Rayleigh remained a centre of political and manorial power for several centuries.

THE MARKET AND THE FAIR

In 1181 Rayleigh was granted a weekly market and in 1227 an annual fair. These were important steps in the growth of the local economy, since they attracted regular business both from within Rayleigh itself and from the surrounding villages.

The market, held in the High Street, was so important that it even affected the layout of the village centre. The wide lower end of the High Street is typical of small country market towns, the width being necessary to

28   Rayleigh High Street, *c*.1910. This wide central street was the ideal place to host a market.

29

29 This photograph seems to have become almost the classic Rayleigh Fair picture, but it illustrates beautifully how the event used to take place in the High Street.

accommodate market stalls either down the middle or along the sides. The narrower, top end of the High Street may also once have been wider, with the land between the High Street and Bellingham Lane (formerly known as Back Lane) originally housing temporary market stalls which later became permanent buildings. The original market died out in the early 19th century, but the modern weekly Wednesday market keeps alive the tradition of Rayleigh as a market town.

The fair, held in the High Street on Trinity Monday (usually late May or early June), was principally a place for the trading of horses and other livestock. On occasions there were over one thousand horses for sale. It was also a place for the hiring of labour and for recreational activities such as sports and other entertainments. It lasted from 1227 to 1899, by which time merriment had taken precedence over trade and it was closed down for being too riotous!

VILLAGE CENTRE
With its market and fair, medieval Rayleigh must have been a busy and bustling place. Over the intervening centuries much has changed in the old village centre, but many buildings

30   One of the earliest known photographs of Rayleigh, dating from 1870.

31   Rayleigh High Street from the tower of Holy Trinity Church, pictured *c*.1915.

32 Holy Trinity Church, *c.*1910. The ivy on the walls was removed as part of a major restoration programme which took place in 1912-14.

from the period remain to give us a feel for what it might have been like. This is perhaps best explained by a tour of the surviving pre-1700 buildings in the village centre, starting with the most significant …

HOLY TRINITY CHURCH

The wide, rising, picturesque High Street of Rayleigh is dominated by Holy Trinity Church.

The current building is almost certainly not the first to have stood on the site. There may have been one here in the Saxon period and there was certainly a church here in the Norman period for Robert de Essex, Lord of the Manor of Rayleigh and founder of Prittlewell Priory, gave to the latter the advowson of Rayleigh church (the right of appointing the incumbent) shortly after the Priory's foundation *c.*1110. Some of the stonework in the current building is of Norman origin. This is particularly evident in the east wall of the chancel, which also

includes some reused Roman brickwork and a blocked up door. The base of an early Norman font, almost certainly the original one, can be seen on display inside the church.

The current building dates mostly from the Perpendicular period (approximately mid-14th to mid-16th centuries), with big, straight, tall windows, making it very light inside. It was begun shortly after 1380, when Aubrey de Vere was Lord of Rayleigh Manor. On the tower above the west door are the remains of seven stone shields depicting the coats-of-arms of different families. The coat-of-arms of de Vere was on the central shield, though this has now unfortunately weathered beyond all recognition.

The nave, chancel and north aisle were the first parts of the building to be constructed. The south aisle was added later. Traces of the windows which were in the original south wall (knocked through to incorporate the south aisle) can still be seen high up above the south

33 The interior of Holy Trinity Church, *c.*1915, before the erection of the screen and the east window, a memorial to the victims of the First World War.

aisle arches. Next to them is a row of stone projections which was evidently provided with the intention of constructing a pitched roof, though a lean-to roof is there now.

At the eastern ends of the aisles are two small chapels. The north chapel, now occupied by the organ, is slightly older than the south. It is thought that this was originally dedicated to St John the Baptist, as an altar dedicated to that saint is mentioned in the will of John Buttell (1496). The choir vestry is accessed via this chapel. It was probably built at the same time, but was later enlarged by the Victorians.

This chapel was probably originally built as a chantry chapel (an endowed chapel where masses for the dead were sung) for Sir John and Lady Thomasine Barrington, who died in 1416 and 1420 respectively and whose tomb was in it. (Sir John is often incorrectly referred to as 'Sir Thomas', which mix-up perhaps originated through confusion with his wife's name.) Sir John was verderer and keeper of Rayleigh

Park, responsible for enforcing Park laws on behalf of the King. A brass commemorating the Barringtons, which was originally on the top of their tomb, can still be seen inside the church.

The south chapel, known as the Alen Chapel, was built in 1517, probably by Richard Alen (or Alleyn) to commemorate his father William, who had died the previous year and had provided the funds for its erection. The grave of William Alen can no longer be seen, but the splendid tomb to Richard, who was also buried in the chapel, survives.

William Alen was owner of Rayleigh Castle and as late as the 19th century maintenance of the south chapel was still the responsibility of the owner of the castle.

Holy Trinity's most impressive external feature is its 70-feet high tower, which dominates the town centre and is a significant landmark for miles around. From the top, one can see the massive transmitter aerial at Kelvedon Hatch near Brentwood and even

34 A brass in Holy Trinity Church of Sir John and
Lady Thomasine Barrington. Their surname survives
in the name of 'Barringtons' which stands opposite
the church. This brass was once on top of their tomb
in the north-east chapel of the church.

35 The tomb of Richard Alen in the south-
east (Alen) chapel of Holy Trinity Church. The
construction of the chapel was financed by Richard's
father, William.

the London landmarks of the Telecom Tower,
NatWest Tower and Canary Wharf, some 30
miles away to the east.

The tower contains eight bells, the oldest
of early 16th-century date and bearing the
maker's mark of Thomas Bullisdon and the
motto 'Sancta Marguereta Ora pro Nos' (St
Margaret, pray for us). An even older bell, now
cracked and unusable, can be seen on display
inside the church. It bears the maker's mark of
Robert Burford (early 15th-century) and the
motto 'Sit Nomen Domini Benedictum' (May
the name of the Lord be blessed).

One of the tower's buttresses (external stone
supports at the base) contains a niche which

almost certainly held a statue, possibly that of
the Virgin Mary. It is thought that such a statue
could have come from a chapel which once
stood at the bottom of London Hill.

Information about this chapel is scarce. The
Essex historian Philip Morant knew of its
existence, writing that 'there was a chapel in
this parish, but where I find not'. However, the
Rochford Hundred historian Philip Benton was
more fortunate, researching at a time when 'the
site of this chapel had been altogether forgotten,
but the foundations have lately been discovered
in a field called the Chapel Field at the bottom
of London Hill to the west of the church'. Floor
tiles were amongst the items found.

It is thought that this chapel was for the use of the priest hired for the chantry (Barrington) chapel mentioned above. The chantry records describe Rayleigh as 'a very great and populous town, having in it the number of 16 score housling people and [many of them living] far from the church'. Its location would have benefited inhabitants in the remoter, western parts of the parish. This is the earliest record of Rayleigh's population, equating to about 300 people.

Also of note externally is the red-brick Tudor porch, a later addition to the original building, dating from the early 16th century.

Much of the church is built of Kentish ragstone, almost certainly brought directly across the Thames by boat. Some of it evidently also came from whatever foundations there were in Rayleigh Castle when Richard II gave permission for his tenants in the village to quarry for stones there in 1394 (see p.12). This grant for quarrying includes the desire 'to repair a certain chapel in the said town [possibly the one at the bottom of London Hill] and to build anew a certain belfry [i.e. the tower]'. Much of the external decoration is provided by flint, the material that brought Stone-Age man to Rayleigh in the first place.

Inside the building there are several features of interest. The rectors' board provides another clue to there having been an earlier church on the site: the first known incumbent, Henry de Saracen, is listed as 1310, some 70 years before the present building was constructed.

Two of the pillars feature ancient inscriptions to 'Roger Smith & Alys his wyf [Alice, his wife]' and Henricus Kendale, the former thought to date from the 15th century. There are further graffiti, of a musical nature, on one of the pillars under the tower.

In the entrance to the organ chapel from the nave stands part of a 15th-century screen which came from Runwell church, near Wickford. It was given to the Rev. Girdlestone Fryer (incumbent 1904-32 and author of two books about Rayleigh) who had it restored and placed there.

Just to the left of this are the rood stairs, a set of stone stairs built into the north wall

36 A bell from the tower of Holy Trinity Church, now cracked and unusable but on display in the church.

which once led to a platform across the top of the chancel arch from where the rector would preach. This platform, known as the rood loft, has long been taken down.

Other items of note include a dug-out chest made from a single block of oak and thought to be up to 800 years old, an 18th-century alms box and the Royal Arms of Queen Anne, dating from c.1702 to c.1707.

The font is dedicated to the memory of Mary Meakens Hilliard, wife of George Hilliard and daughter of Thomas Brewitt junior of Down Hall.

Amongst the church's treasures not normally on display are the chalice, paten and flagon (goblet, plate and container for wine), the former two dating from around 1683 and the latter from 1718. The flagon was given to the church by the Rev. Edward Roberts (rector 1702-18).

The churchyard contains several gravestones of interest. These include a headstone with a skull and crossbones standing next to the south chapel which commemorates the life of Rebeckah Merryfield, who died in 1730 at the age of 38. The Essex Society for Family History documented all the graves at the church in 1992, so a complete record exists for posterity.

37 The rood stairs at Holy Trinity Church, which gave access to the rood loft (a platform from which sermons would be preached) and which were discovered during the 1912-14 restoration.

39 The Victorian font at Holy Trinity Church, dedicated to the memory of Mary Meakens Hilliard, daughter of Thomas Brewitt junior and wife of Dr George Hilliard.

38 An oak chest at Holy Trinity Church, said to be 800 years old.

Between 1912 and 1914 a major restoration project was carried out at the church. Ivy was removed from the exterior and plaster was taken off the ceiling to reveal the beams. It was during this period that the rood stairs were rediscovered, hidden behind plaster. Rotten pews were replaced with chairs, a gallery at the west end was removed and the floor was repaired. The architect Edmund Sedding, a church specialist, oversaw the work.

Further restoration work took place in 1969, and in 1976 the church hall to the north of the church was opened. However, the biggest and most controversial 20th-century project was the construction of the Parish Centre, which involved the reopening of the blocked

40 A sketch of Rayleigh rectory, showing how it looked *c.*1915. The Rectory was demolished in 1967.

north doorway and the construction of a new building linking the church to the church hall. It was officially opened by the Bishop of Chelmsford on 18 February 1995.

One of the most recent improvements was the remodelling of the church entrance in 2003 to improve access and open up a view of the interior for those entering the building.

THE RECTORY

The rectory for Holy Trinity stood just to the north-east of the church in what is now Rectory Garth. William White, writing in 1848, described it as 'a spacious rectory house, with tasteful grounds and 39 acres of Glebe'. In 1932 Reverend Fryer wrote of its 'big sweep of lawn and the background of fine old trees …'.

The building was 16th century or earlier, with later alterations and additions. It had a central block, with north and south crosswings, the upper storey of the south wing originally projecting over the lower storey on the east side.

The building was demolished in 1967 as it was becoming too expensive to maintain.

BARRINGTONS

Another building of great age and historical interest is Barringtons, which stands at the junction of Hockley Road and Webster's Way on the site of the one-time home of the Barrington (or Barenton) family, keepers of Rayleigh Park. The family is thought to have originated from Barrington in Cambridgeshire but, as Benton

41   Barringtons, named after the Barrington family, now a solicitor's office. A side extension houses the Rochford District Council council chamber.

says, 'whether they gave this place the name or derived their own therefrom is unknown'.

The Essex branch of the family resided chiefly at Hatfield Broad Oak, where there is still a Barrington Hall. The first Rayleigh Barrington was Sir Philip, grandfather of the Sir John Barrington referred to above who is commemorated in Rayleigh church.

42   Barringtons Cottages, showing Rayleigh market, the modern-day successor to the old one which was held in the High Street.

The family is said to have died out locally in the early 16th century, though a Richard Barrington (connection unknown) was rector of Holy Trinity in 1678.

The current building, which dates primarily from the mid-to-late 17th century but has a later facade, replaced the building the Barringtons would have known. The facade was added in the 19th century by Daniel Nash, who renamed the building Rayleigh Place, a name which did not last. It was described in a sales advertisement attributed to 1835 as 'a handsome, newly-erected, white-brick-fronted villa'. Other notable 19th-century owners included Thomas Brewitt, Dr George Hilliard, Dr Jonas Asplin and William Cross, a local brewer.

Barringtons is now in the occupation of Simpson, Robertson and Edgington (solicitors), whilst later extensions house the Community Information Centre and the Rayleigh offices of Rochford District Council.

43 91 High Street, currently occupied by Size Up. The right-hand end of this building dates back to the 14th century, making it the oldest known surviving secular building in Rayleigh.

Close by can be seen the 18th-century, timber-framed and weatherboarded Barringtons Cottages, which occupy the site of cottages which once housed workers who maintained Rayleigh Park. These have been converted to commercial use and are home to a ski and snowboard shop.

OTHER PRE-1700 BUILDINGS IN THE VILLAGE CENTRE

The oldest proven surviving secular building in Rayleigh is 91 High Street, parts of which have been dated to *c.*1350. This building, currently occupied by Size Up but probably better remembered as Sansom's gentlemen's outfitters or the North Thames Gas Board (the two previous occupiers), was shown by an archaeological survey in 1989 to have been built in two parts.

The southernmost part is the oldest and is thought to have been the south wing of an open medieval hall house, with possibly a north wing to match it on the other side of the central hall. The northern part of the current building, which occupies the site of the presumed hall, dates from the late 16th or early 17th centuries. It may have been about this time that the building was converted from residential use to commercial.

From at least 1861 to 1881 the building was occupied by John Belcham, a draper. By the early 1900s the southern part was occupied by the Westminster Bank, whilst the northern part was a haberdashery and soft furnisher's. The building was also occupied for a long period by Percy Deveson, a draper. The existing Georgian-style bowed shop windows date from the 1930s.

Another building of note is the one now designated 42a and 42b High Street, at the junction of High Street and Bellingham Lane, which currently houses Atkinson Sportsworld and TK's. This building is, however, better known as Mann's. The building dates from

44   Rayleigh High Street, *c*.1900, showing on the left what became the shop of H. Mann and Son, from which this junction of the High Street and Bellingham Lane (left) became known as 'Mann's Corner'.

at least the 16th century, though the brick facing is later.

Plans to demolish this building in late 1970 caused great controversy. Much of historic Rayleigh was being demolished at the time and Mann's was both ancient and occupied a prominent site. The decision to retain it has been described as 'probably the turning point in the fight to retain old buildings in the High Street'.

On the opposite side of the road, further up towards the church, is 11 High Street (Squire's tea and coffee shop). This is also of at least 16th-century origin, while 9 High Street next door (La Romantica restaurant) probably dates from the 17th century.

Further up, just off the High Street at 1-5 Church Street, are Wern Cottages. These too are of at least 17th-century date.

At the other end of Church Street, at 13-17 London Hill, are three 17th-century cottages known collectively as 'Mount Pleasant'. Although now separate dwellings, these were formerly one house.

The *Crown* is the oldest surviving public house in the village centre, dating from the late 17th or early 18th century, with later additions. During the 18th and early 19th centuries it was a coaching inn and one of the main staging posts on the route into south-east Essex from London. It was also the meeting place of the local hunt.

THE DUTCH COTTAGE

One other building worthy of attention at this stage is the Dutch Cottage in Crown Hill.

This distinctive thatched, octagonal building (officially 33 Crown Hill) bears the date '1621', but it seems from constructional evidence actually to date from some time after 1700, probably *c*.1740.

Quite why it was erected in Rayleigh is unclear. It is similar to two more well-known Dutch cottages on nearby Canvey Island, one of which is also dated '1621', and it is thought that one of the Rayleigh Dutch Cottage's 19th-century occupants simply copied the date from the similar-looking Canvey building!

45   Rayleigh High Street, *c*.1915, showing on the extreme left the buildings which are now La Romantica restaurant and Squire's Coffee Shop, two of the oldest surviving buildings in the town centre. Another old (but newer) building, Kingsleigh House, stands next to them (see p.55).

46   London Hill, *c*.1915, showing on the left the Mount Pleasant Cottages.

47 The *Crown Hotel*, always one of the principal hostelries in the town. Note the narrowness of the gap between the *Crown* and the neighbouring building on the extreme left of the picture. This is the top of Crown Hill, now much wider (and busier) following the demolition of the buildings on the opposite side of the Hill from the pub.

48 The Dutch Cottage in Crown Hill in the early 20th century. The other building shown – the only other one in existence in the area at the time – is Sweep's Row, which was demolished in the 1930s.

The building is 'Dutch' because it is of typical 17th-century Dutch design. The buildings were octagonal or circular to give them added strength on their usually marshland base and the superstitious Dutch believed that the lack of corners meant that the Devil had no place to hide!

Forty-seven Dutch Delft tiles, the oldest dating from the 17th century, were found inside the building during restoration work in the early 1980s. These could have belonged to a 19th-century occupant, Naomi Hurrell, who was born in one of the Canvey cottages and lived in the Rayleigh one with her husband and nine children! It may have been Mrs Hurrell who attributed a Dutch identity to the cottage.

During the 19th century the building was known as Octagon Cottage or The Round House. It is said to have been home to the keeper of the Essex Union foxhounds, but the evidence for this is inconclusive.

In 1870 the cottage was purchased by William Pissey, a man of many parts who was a chemist, newsagent, stationer, insurance agent and major property owner in the village. Pissey never lived in the cottage, but let it out to tenants, such as the Hurrells. After a successful business career he died in 1883 and is buried in the churchyard at Holy Trinity. The cottage remained in the family's ownership until the early 1900s.

In the first part of the 20th century the cottage was owned by Edwin Sparrow. From the First World War to the early 1930s it went through a succession of owners, including Mrs K.B. Lamb, who sold it to Mrs Parker, who wanted to open tea rooms there. However, shortly afterwards it was acquired by Richard Wakelin, a draper, who bought it to save it from falling into disrepair. He owned it until 1958, by which time its historical significance had been recognised and it had been officially designated as a listed building.

In 1958 it was sold to J.T. Byford and Sons, a well-known local firm of builders. In 1964, following the launch of a public subscription

49   Restoration work at the Dutch Cottage in the early 1980s.

campaign the previous year, it was sold to Rayleigh Urban District Council (UDC) to be 'preserved as an amenity and showplace for the district'. Rochford District Council, successors to the UDC, carried out a full restoration which was completed in 1984.

The building was re-thatched in February 2004 by S.A. Shelley.

It is open on Wednesday afternoons by appointment.

THE RAYLEIGH MARTYRS
Amongst the earliest recorded incidents in the life of Rayleigh village are two horrifying ones – the burnings of two Protestants in the High Street for their religious beliefs. The events took place in 1555 during the reign of the Catholic Queen Mary – the height of Protestant persecution.

50 William Pissey, pictured *c.*1880 in Masonic regalia. Pissey had a wide range of entrepreneurial interests in the Victorian town, was the first president of the Rayleigh branch of the Masons and also once owned the Dutch Cottage.

51 The re-thatching of the Dutch Cottage in February 2004.

52 The unveiling ceremony for the Martyrs' Memorial in September 1908. It looks as if most of the town turned out to witness the event.

On 26 March 1555 Thomas Causton, a gentleman of the neighbouring parish of Thundersley, was consigned to the flames on a charge of heresy, essentially for not accepting the doctrines of the Catholic Church. He, and a fellow prisoner, Thomas Higbed of Horndon-on-the-Hill, were tried and found guilty together. Higbed was taken to Horndon to meet his death, Causton to Rayleigh.

Three months later, on 10 June 1555, John Ardeley, a husbandman of Great Wigborough (some 20 miles to the north-east of Rayleigh between Maldon and Colchester) suffered a similar fate. A fellow villager, John Simson, was also convicted, being taken to Rochford

to meet his death on the same day. It seems likely that they were brought to south-east Essex because the Rochford Hundred was something of a hotbed of Protestantism and Rochford and Rayleigh were the two largest towns in the Hundred.

On 23 September 1908, 'with a view of perpetuating the names and memories of these sainted martyrs', a memorial was erected in the High Street, almost opposite Crown Hill, as close as possible to the believed site of the martyrdoms. It commemorates Causton and Ardeley, plus two other local men – Robert Drakes, minister of Thundersley, and William Tyms, curate of Hockley – who were consigned to the flames together at Smithfield in London on 24 April 1556.

VILLAGE LIFE

Some of the earliest glimpses into everyday village life in Rayleigh are provided by the parish registers, which go back to 1548.

These registers reveal, for example, that in 1631 the wife of the then rector, the Reverend Stephen Vassall, was exceptionally granted permission in Lent 'to eat flesh so long as her sickness shall continue'.

During his incumbency, the Reverend Vassall made a perambulation to record the line of the Rayleigh parish boundary (in a ceremony known as 'beating the bounds'). The record he made was used by later rectors during two court cases over the ownership of a wood which the occupants of a neighbouring parish tried unsuccessfully to claim for themselves.

In June 1640 a Rayleigh innkeeper, Thomas Read, had a case of smallpox on his premises but, for fear of losing trade, deliberately kept it secret. One child died of this highly infectious disease and several other people caught it. Rayleigh inhabitants subsequently petitioned the authorities to prevent Read from keeping inns in the future.

In 1643 the Reverend Vassall was succeeded as rector of Holy Trinity by Abraham Caley, a controversial minister who was ejected from the living for refusing to comply with the 1662 Act of Uniformity and thereby dissenting from the practices and doctrines of the established church. He is said to have held his own prayer meetings in what became known as Meeting House Lane (now Castle Road) after his ejection. An intelligent man, conversant with eight languages and author of a religious work, *A Glimpse of Eternity*, Caley was befriended by the wife of the 4th Earl of Warwick at Rochford Hall. Her diary records that she travelled to Rayleigh to see him, welcomed him into her Rochford home and was 'much moved' by his death.

Caley died in 1672. He is remembered in the Caley Memorial Hall next to the United Reformed Church in Crown Hill.

In the late 1650s, during Caley's incumbency, banns of marriage were published in the market place and signed by a justice of the peace.

Caley was succeeded by the Reverend Samuel Bull, his nephew, who in turn was succeeded by Richard Barrington.

Barrington's successor, John Duffe, proved as controversial as Caley, being deprived of the living in 1682 for 'turning Roman Catholic'. His successor, the Reverend John Smith, met exactly the same fate in 1690. These events took place against a backdrop of national hysteria about the potential overthrow of England by Catholics and events at Rayleigh at this time clearly reflected the national mood.

The Rev. Smith was succeeded by the Rev. Hugo Pyne who in turn was succeeded in 1692 by the Rev. Dr John Luke. Also in 1692 there is a record of one George Dearsley being buried in linen, a move designed to try to prop up the ailing English cloth industry.

The right of appointing the incumbent at Rayleigh Church had originally been vested in Prittlewell Priory, but this ceased in 1536 when the Priory was dissolved. After this the advowson appears to have been vested in the owner of Rayleigh Manor, which included successively Lord Hunsdon, the Rich/Warwick family and the Bristows. In 1610 there was a parsonage house, a barn, a stable, gardens, an orchard and about four acres of glebe (land belonging to the Church). The glebe land was increased to about 40 acres by 1702.

In 1686 there was sufficient accommodation in the town for 70 visitors and 100 horses.

Six

On the Map

❖

In 1576 Rayleigh appeared on the earliest detailed map of Essex, that of cartographical pioneer Christopher Saxton, a land surveyor. Saxton's map, however, was very simplistic and nothing of the village was shown except the name (spelt 'Raleghe') and the church.

Over the next hundred years maps increased in both detail and scale and the local road network became much more accurately depicted. This was important because, as the road network grew, Rayleigh became the focal point of several major roads. Its geographical position effectively made it the gateway to the Rochford Hundred and through it was obtained access to the villages to the east of the Rayleigh Hills.

The roads themselves were also improving, gradually developing from badly maintained dirt tracks into more substantial roads that could carry wheeled vehicles.

THE LOCAL ROAD NETWORK

The main road from London – which wound its way into south-east Essex via Shenfield,

53 London Road, *c.*1905, showing the approach to Rayleigh. This was historically the main road from the Capital to the town. The landmarks of the church, windmill and Mount can clearly be seen at the top right.

54   London Hill, *c.*1915, when it was still virtually a country lane. This was historically the main approach into the town centre from the west. The cottages on the left are still there.

55   Church Street in August 1900. Surely, a welcome sight to old-time travellers to Rayleigh from London as they had only to turn the corner by the church and they would finally be in the High Street after their long journey.

56   Hockley Road, *c.*1915, showing Holly Cottage. The cottage is now in Wat Tyler Country Park at Pitsea, where it forms part of a display of traditional Essex buildings.

57 Hockley Road, showing the junction with Hambro Hill, *c.*1930. The fields have now been replaced by housing.

58 The High Road, with the *Paul Pry* on the left.

59 Another picture of the High Road, *c.*1915, this time further down towards Great Wheatley Road.

Billericay and Wickford – entered Rayleigh from a north-westerly direction at the top end of the High Street via London Road, London Hill and Church Street. Travellers bound for destinations beyond Rayleigh then had a choice of routes as the road from London split into two.

Those heading for Rochford went north-eastwards along Hockley Road, which followed the ridge of the Rayleigh Hills. Those heading for Leigh went south through the High Street and High Road to Rayleigh Road (named 'Rayleigh' from a Hadleigh perspective) and up to what is now the A13. At the southern end of the High Street, this latter road branched eastwards to Eastwood and Daws Heath.

The routes became well-established and the modern road network is still based on them.

60   Rayleigh from the Eastwood Road in 1900. The fledgling town is still concentrated around the High Street area which is still surrounded by fields.

61   Eastwood Road, looking east from the corner of Daws Heath Road, c.1914. It would not be possible to herd cows in the road nowadays!

62   Eastwood Road at the corner of White House Chase, c.1910.

63   Daws Heath Road, pictured probably around the end of the First World War.

64 Rayleigh High Street, showing on the right the *Golden Lion*, once the principal hostelry in the town. The ironmongery on the left was one of several properties in Rayleigh owned by T.W. Finch. The building in front of the church was best known as Patmore's bakery. It also housed Rayleigh's first telephone exchange. It was demolished in the 1930s.

ROAD MAINTENANCE

In the early days of highway maintenance the repair of each stretch of road was the responsibility of the landowner whose property it bordered. Not all landowners took this responsibility seriously and roads were consequently often poorly maintained.

The Highways Act of 1555 sought to resolve this by removing the responsibility for the upkeep of roads from such landowners and introducing instead the concept of all local people being responsible for the upkeep of local roads. Each parish had to elect two highway surveyors to monitor the condition of local roads and every family had either to pay for labourers to carry out any necessary repairs or do the work themselves. As wheeled vehicles became increasingly common this became quite a burdensome task.

To resolve some of the impracticalities of this form of road-mending, the concept of toll-roads or turnpikes was introduced, whereby those using the road paid a fee to do so and were consequently the ones who paid for its upkeep. This was a much better arrangement where the main roads were concerned because villagers living on routes used by hundreds of non-locals would otherwise find themselves paying ridiculously large sums for the upkeep of roads to the benefit of others. The first turnpikes began to appear in the late 17th century, but it was the 18th century that was the golden age of turnpike construction.

A first-hand account of Rayleigh roads in this period was provided by the Methodist preacher, John Wesley, who visited nearby Leigh-on-Sea several times between 1748 and 1756. On one such visit in 1755 he recorded that 'when we were about two miles short of Rayleigh … the ruts were so deep and uneven that the horses could scarce stand,

and the chaise was continually in danger of overturning'.

In Rayleigh, the main road from London and the two branch roads to Rochford and Leigh were constituted as turnpike roads by Act of Parliament in 1747 under the control of the Essex Turnpike Trust, the largest such company in the county. Trust meetings took place in the town at the now-gone *Golden Lion* inn, the most prestigious hostelry of the period. This stood on the east side of the High Street and was known at various periods as the *Lion* and the *Red Lion*. Manorial courts were held there, plus various commercial meetings and associated functions. It ceased trading in 1929 and was demolished after the Second World War.

The *Golden Lion*, the *Crown* and other businesses associated with road transport (carriers, blacksmiths, wheelwrights, etc.) all prospered following the creation of the turnpike road. Regular coach services were established between Rochford and London and by the 1820s it was possible to make the journey to the Capital and back in one day – a great improvement in the speed of travel.

By the 1830s, however, new legislation, improved road surfaces and increasing debts for many turnpike companies led Parliament to consider ending the turnpike system, as turnpikes and their charges were becoming increasingly unpopular.

In 1841 Rayleigh residents called for a meeting to oppose 'the case of the Trustees of the Roads having given notice of their intention to erect tollbars or gates in the town'.

The 1840s saw a reorganisation of the Trust in an attempt to cut down on costs, but the advent of the railways in that same decade was to be the turnpikes' death-knell. In 1856 the opening of the London, Tilbury & Southend railway and the consequent reduction in road traffic had a drastic effect on the profitability of the south-east Essex roads. It was said that in the late 1850s one could stand for an hour in the middle of the once-busy Rayleigh-Rochford turnpike road and not see a single soul!

There was still time for a few opposition missiles to be launched. In 1851 a meeting chaired by George Belcham 'resolved that the new gates, if erected at Rayleigh as proposed, will be a great nuisance and injury to the town and neighbourhood'. This would have meant that there would be seven turnpike gates within four miles of the town, with the existing ones already operating 'very much to the injury of the inhabitants'.

The local turnpike roads were finally killed off in 1864 with the formation of the Rochford Highway Board under the 1862 Highways Act. This new Board was responsible for the highways in a newly-constituted Rochford Highway District (covering the Rochford Hundred parishes). The Essex Turnpike Trust was wound up in 1866 and highways management and road maintenance passed to the new Highways Board.

CHAPMAN AND ANDRÉ

It was during the peak of turnpike prosperity that the best early map of the county was produced. John Chapman and Peter André's 1777 map was on a larger scale (two inches to one mile) than any previous one, showing road layouts, woodland and even individual buildings.

In Rayleigh the principal transport arteries of London Road, London Hill, Hockley Road, Eastwood Road, the High Road, the High Street, Church Street, Bellingham Lane, Down Hall Road, Hambro Hill, Bull Lane, Daws Heath Road, Castle Road, Great Wheatley Road and Love Lane are all clearly visible. The only major roads yet to appear are Crown Hill (originally called Crown Lane and then simply a narrow track ending in fields) and Webster's Way (late 20th-century).

The castle, the church and the manor houses of Great Wheatley, Little Wheatley, Down Hall and Harberges are all shown, as are Little (Rayleigh) Lodge and Eastwood Lodge. White House Farm, Lovetts Lodge (off Rawreth Lane and now called Lubard's Lodge) and Turret House (off Hockley Road) are also shown, as are Lime House and Rivers.

In 1824 White House Farm was the property of John Sweeting. In the 1840s it was owned by William Stonehewer and occupied by John Lamprell. The best-known 20th-century owner was the Flack family.

In the mid-19th century Turret House was occupied by John and Lydia Page. Later it was owned by Thomas William Offin, previously of Down Hall. Both men served as churchwardens at Holy Trinity and Mr Offin was a worshipper there for over 50 years. There are commemorative plaques to both of them inside the church.

Lime House, which stood at the extreme eastern end of Rayleigh parish where Eastwood Road, Rayleigh becomes Rayleigh Road, Eastwood, is remembered in the name 'Lime House Hill' and in the 'Lime House Nurseries', behind the Wyevale garden centre. It was owned in 1840 by William Stonehewer and occupied by Thomas Horner.

Rivers, later known as Holly Trees or Hull Trees, stood in the High Road just north of Rayleigh Weir in the vicinity of Orchard Avenue and is mentioned in early 19th-century

65 Chapman & André's map of Rayleigh from 1777. This was the first reasonably accurate large-scale map of the town and includes many of the roads and buildings mentioned in the text.

66 Bull Lane, pictured between the wars.

67 The milestone at Drovers Hill on the Rayleigh-Hockley border, which is marked, along with other milestones, on Chapman & André's map (above).

68   White House Farm. The farmhouse survives, despite the development of the surrounding farmland.

travel guides as a reference point on the coach journey from London to Southend.

Stevens Farm, to the north-east of the village centre just to the south of Hockley Woods, is also shown on the map, though not actually named. This and neighbouring Fisher's Farm were once known as Upper and Lower Parkgate Farms respectively. Stevens Farm was probably named after a Rayleigh glover *c.*1577. In the

69   Stevens Farm, historically known as Upper Parkgate Farm, which is one of the several surviving working farms in Rayleigh.

late 18th and early 19th centuries it was owned by the Crosier family. In 1840 it was occupied by Matthias Wendon. Several members of the Wendon family were farmers here and at White House Farm.

EIGHTEENTH-CENTURY RAYLEIGH

Despite all the transport activity and the increasing number of travellers, Rayleigh's position as the most significant village in the Hundred had by now been lost. By the 18th century this honour had passed to Rochford, which was more central and was the market town for the remote, outlying, agricultural parishes to the east. It was also the main destination of the northern turnpike road and the start/finish point for coach services to London. The presence of the Rich family must also have helped increase Rochford's importance.

By 1768 the Essex historian, Philip Morant, was describing Rayleigh as having 'grown much

70   Pearson's Farm in London Road.

ruinous and decayed' compared with its former grandeur.

This feeling of decline persisted early into the next century with George Cooke, a traveller, writing *c*.1810 that 'the now inconsiderable village of Rayleigh was once a market town of no small importance … [but] at present it is only remarkable for the remains of a strongly fortified castle'. Of the route between Billericay and Rayleigh, Cooke wrote that 'we meet with nothing particularly interesting'.

INTERESTING BUILDINGS
Apart from those already mentioned, several other surviving buildings in Rayleigh had appeared by the end of the 18th century.

The pair of black, weatherboarded cottages at 64-66 London Hill dates from the early 18th century, or possibly the late 17th. The left-hand cottage has had a later shopfront fitted.

In London Road, Pearson's Farm is also early 18th-century and of classic timber-framed and weatherboarded design. In 1840 it was owned by Mary Pearson but occupied by James Richmond. In that year Richmond also occupied a farm on the site of the old Rayleigh Castle.

In the High Street, the three-storey Kingsleigh House dates from the 1790s and was built on the site of an old coaching inn called the *Bull*, itself said to have dated from at least 1560 and to have had a bull-baiting garden in the grounds. Kingsleigh House is now offices, in the occupation of Todman's Solicitors and other local businesses.

Round the corner in Hockley Road numbers 18, 24 and 56 all date from this period. No. 50 Hockley Road may be earlier (see below).

At the other end of the town, near Rayleigh Weir, is Weir Farm, a white, weatherboarded

71   Hockley Road, *c*.1915. The building on the right, Fern House, is now officially No 18. Two buildings to the left is No 24. Both are of 18th-century date. The cottage in between has now disappeared.

building dating from *c*.1700. It took its name from a nearby weir and in turn gave it to the later road junction. It was occupied in the 1840s and 1850s by James Richmond, whose wife Susanna took over the running of the farm after his death. By 1910 it was occupied by Newman Clemance.

72   Weir Farm, an old but often overlooked building at the southern end of the town (and parish). It stands right next to the important Rayleigh Weir road interchange, but is surprisingly inconspicuous despite the busy location.

A 'lost' Rayleigh building worth mentioning is Holly Cottage (see illustration 56), a 300-year-old weatherboarded structure which was moved to Wat Tyler Country Park in Pitsea, five miles away! Here, with other similar buildings from Takeley, it now forms an educational resource for schoolchildren.

WINDMILLS

Chapman and André's map shows two windmills in Rayleigh, not surprising for a hilltop village. These, and the surviving later windmill, were three of at least five windmills in the town.

The mill shown in Hockley Road (above the word 'Raleigh' [*sic*]) would become known as 'Ruffle's Mill' after an early 19th-century tenant, Benjamin Ruffle. Ruffle lived in a house in front of the mill at what is now 50 Hockley Road, whilst the windmill stood on a mound behind what is now 62 Hockley Road.

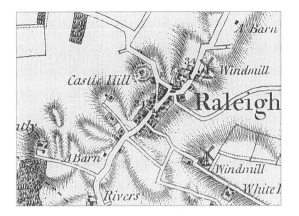

73 A close-up of the windmills on Chapman & André's map, 1777.

74 Ruffles in Hockley Road, once home to the Rayleigh miller, Benjamin Ruffle.

When the mill was built is not known, but it was owned by the Hurrell family from at least the 1730s to the early 1790s, though often occupied and run by tenants. During Ruffle's tenancy it was owned by William Audley, a successful local businessman and property owner. The two men evidently had a good relationship, for Ruffle married Audley's

daughter, Elizabeth and, when Audley died in 1829, the Ruffles inherited. For how long they worked the mill after this is not known, but it is believed to have survived until the late 1860s.

No. 50 Hockley Road is thought to date back to the 17th century. No. 56 Hockley Road, a white, thatched, weatherboarded

75 The graves of Benjamin Ruffle and William Audley, 19th-century Rayleigh millers, now lying next to each other in Holy Trinity churchyard.

76 The surviving Rayleigh windmill, of a type known as a tower mill, pictured in the early 20th century.

cottage, probably dating from the 18th century, is believed to be the former mill cottage.

The second windmill on Chapman and André's map stood on the north side of Eastwood Road in the vicinity of Picton Gardens. It was actually one of a pair of mills, the second of which did not appear until *c.*1793. Because of these associations, Eastwood Road was previously known as Mill Lane and Two Mills Lane.

The Audley family also had connections with these windmills and, after William Audley's death, they were run for two years by his wife, Elizabeth, and then by two of his daughters, Rachel and Sarah Ann. The mills were still in the ownership of a Mary Ann Audley in the early 1880s, though often occupied and worked by tenants. They were dismantled *c.*1884.

A fourth lost windmill is shown on a map of 1825 a little to the north-east of Little Wheatley Farm. Apart from its appearance on this map, which could be in error, nothing else is known about it.

The fifth and final known Rayleigh windmill is the one which survives today.

Conflicting dates are given locally for the construction of this mill (usually 1798 and 1809), but the acknowledged Essex windmill expert, Kenneth Farries, dates it at the latter. It stands in what was the outer bailey of Rayleigh Castle, which by this time was part of a landholding known as Castle Farm. In June 1809, according to Farries, Thomas Higgs, a Rayleigh timber merchant, bought a plot of land on the farm and erected the windmill on it. Higgs is mentioned in the minutes of the parish vestry (the local authority of its day) in 1810 in respect of a lease agreement between himself and the vestry. Unfortunately, however, Higgs' business was not successful and sale notices soon appeared in local newspapers.

One of these was on 20 December 1816 in the *Chelmsford Chronicle*. This advertised the auction of the windmill by Messrs Bellingham and Hurrell at the *Golden Lion* on the forthcoming New Year's Day on behalf of the trustees of Thomas Higgs. There were two lots: 'a very valuable freehold estate' incorporating the 'newly-erected' windmill and an adjoining estate 'comprising a comfortable dwelling-house and baking-office'. The windmill was said to have been 'built in the most substantial manner, with the very best materials, no expense being spared'. It was 'allowed by judges to be one of the best built mills in the county of Essex', standing 'extremely well winded, and in the most luxuriant corn country, at an agreeable distance from the principal market towns'. Five new cottages were included in the windmill lot, plus 'an inexhaustible quantity of fine tile and brick earth'. Clearly not wishing to be accused of understatement, Bellingham and

77 Another photograph of the surviving Rayleigh mill, this time through the lens of George Dawson. The photograph was taken on 29 August 1900.

78 A photograph of the interior of the windmill, showing some of the exhibits housed in the museum there.

79 Another photograph of museum exhibits at the windmill.

Hurrell concluded their advertisement by saying that 'without even fearing the charge of exaggeration from the most competent judges, the auctioneers venture to state that the above is one of the best windmills in the whole eastern district, whether viewed as to situation, construction or durability'.

The windmill was bought by William Hart of Woodham Mortimer, who was still the owner in 1840 though the mill was being worked by Benjamin Ruffle.

After Hart, the mill was worked successively by George Britton and his sons, John and Samuel, and then by Thomas Brown. T.J. Brown & Sons became very successful and continued to operate into the 1930s. By 1900 the mill was being worked for them by a well-known local miller, Mr Crabbe.

The use of the sails was discontinued c.1906, but the mill continued to be worked by steam, diesel and then electricity for another 30 years. The cap and sails were removed and the tower was crowned with decorative battlements. In 1909 the wooden platform around the mill, which was used by the miller to attend to the sails, was also removed.

The windmill stood neglected and sail-less until the early 1970s when recognition of its value as a historic building encouraged local people to try to restore it. Rayleigh Urban District Council and the Rayleigh & District Antiquarian & Natural History Society (now the Rayleigh Historical Society) together set up a small museum on the ground floor which opened for business on 16 May 1970. In 1972 campaigners launched an appeal to put up new sails and this was accomplished by the autumn of 1974. The wooden platform was also replaced.

This achievement was, as Kenneth Farries observed, 'a minor triumph for the preservationists over the redevelopers who have removed so much of the old core of the settlement'.

The windmill is one of the most distinctive landmarks on the Rayleigh Hills ridge and together with the castle mound and the church provides what the eminent architectural historian, Sir Nikolaus Pevsner, called the 'three visual and historical accents' of the town. He reserved particular praise for the windmill, describing it as 'a visually successful landmark'.

At the time of writing the windmill is open on Saturday mornings from April to September for access to the ground floor museum only, but there are plans afoot to develop it further as a 21st-century tourist attraction. Two lottery bids have been turned down, but in November 2004 £340,000 was provided by the Thames Gateway project to revamp it. This may include provision of a new museum, access to the upper floors, an observation gallery and cameras for the disabled. The National Trust, owner of the nearby castle, is amongst several bodies said to be keen to be involved.

CHURCH AND VILLAGE LIFE

In 1702 the Reverend Edward Roberts was appointed by Robert Bristow as rector of Holy Trinity Church. Roberts was an active and conscientious incumbent, carrying out his own 'beating the bounds' perambulations and recording in detail in the parish registers much about everyday Rayleigh life.

On 26 November 1703 Roberts recorded that Rayleigh was struck by what became known as 'The Channel Storm', 'a violent storm which did very great damage both by sea and land' and killed an estimated 8,000 people throughout England. Ships were sunk off the Essex coast and many buildings were damaged, including Roberts' rectory and barn.

In May 1705, the Rev. Roberts, churchwardens Henry Hackett and Charles Bunchley and

several parishioners carried out a perambulation of the eastern parish boundary, marking its line at various points as they went. A similar perambulation of the western side was carried out in May 1708.

In July 1711 the Bishop of London, Dr Henry Compton, visited Holy Trinity and confirmed 300 people from Rayleigh and the surrounding area. Many local clergymen were in attendance.

With the increasing road network and associated traffic it is not surprising to find two highways surveyors mentioned in the registers: John Parnill and Thomas Wood in 1711-12.

In 1715 the Rev. Roberts wrote that 'on Tuesday March 6 between 7 and 8 o'clock in the evening were seen meteors or fiery apparitions which caused a terror to all beholders and … that terrible appearance continued more or less all that night'. What the inhabitants of Rayleigh saw is not known but it could have been the Northern Lights. The rector recorded a total eclipse of the sun in the same year.

On 26 May 1715 the Rev. Roberts, Henry Cockerton and Thomas Merryfield met to walk the parish boundary. A detailed report is given in the records.

The Rev. Roberts also gave some material gifts to the church, including the communion cup and tankard.

The Rev. Roberts died in 1718 and was buried beneath a brick altar tomb to the north of the church, now in the central courtyard following the addition of the Parish Centre in the 1990s.

The job of following Roberts was given to the Reverend Arthur Ashley Sykes, who went on to become one of Rayleigh's longest-serving incumbents, remaining in the post for nearly 40 years. His grandfather and great-grandfather had both been clergymen in neighbouring Hertfordshire.

Sykes came to Rayleigh from a position in Cambridgeshire and he seems to have been well thought of in ecclesiastical circles, holding several posts simultaneously. Whilst he was at Rayleigh he was also assistant preacher at St James Church in Westminster, Doctor

80 The grave of the Rev. Edward Roberts on the north side of the church, now within the courtyard area created by the building of the Parish Centre in 1995 and not normally visible to members of the public.

in Divinity at the University of Cambridge, Dean of St Burien in Cornwall and Prebend at a church in Winchester. Curates operated in Rayleigh whenever Sykes was absent elsewhere, but he stayed in the village every summer when his commitments elsewhere allowed.

Sykes was a learned and intelligent man, having been educated at St Paul's School in London and then at Cambridge University. He is said to have published 63 works between 1712 and 1757 and for many years these resided in the vestry at Rayleigh. Benton described him as 'a hearty friend to liberty of conscience and the free toleration of every religious opinion … of gentle and obliging manners, unsoured by controversy, just, humane to the poor, exact and punctual in his payments … [and] careful in the choice of a substitute when absent from town'. He died in November 1756 and was buried at St James Church, Westminster. A portrait of Sykes painted when he was in his forties is said to have been given by his widow to Holy Trinity's patron, Robert Bristow.

Sykes seems to have been more formal in his record-keeping than the Rev. Roberts, using the parish registers for their main intended purpose of recording births, marriages and deaths. Nevertheless, his records continue to give an insight into village life. In 1718, for example, the burial of 'a stranger', Martha

Jackson, took place. In 1751 John Cock, 'officer of excise', was interred.

From January to August 1753 there were 29 burials in Rayleigh, 25 of them from smallpox, a highly infectious disease. It was still present in April 1763 when there was another outbreak, with several fatalities. However, the village was clear of the disease by 16 May, which was just as well because the fair, which would bring more people into the village, took place on 30 May.

In 1787 the authorities in neighbouring Rawreth parish resolved to inoculate local poor people, including those in Rayleigh, in an attempt to check the spread of the disease. This was to be carried out by William Dobson.

Arthur Sykes was succeeded as rector of Rayleigh by his brother George, who held the incumbency at nearby Hawkwell. George Sykes died in 1766 and left much of his fortune to Robert Bristow's son as a mark of gratitude for Bristow's patronage both of himself and his brother/predecessor, Arthur.

Stephen Waller and then Charles Wright succeeded the Sykes brothers. In 1798 the Rev. Wright recorded that

> Alexander Gibbon, mast maker, Execution Dock, Wapping, London, in grateful remembrance … of having married Mary, daughter of the late Rev. Daniel Halloway, many years curate of this parish, presented the flagstaff and St George's Ensign; which was hoisted for the first time upon the news of Lord Nelson's victory at The Nile, August 1st 1798, upon the tower of this church.

Wright was often absent from Rayleigh and the parish was looked after by curates, including the Rev. Miles Moor.

The Rev. Wright was succeeded in 1799 by Reverend Sir John Head. Head, like Arthur Sykes, was to hold the post for nearly 40 years, but for half this time Rayleigh was looked after by a curate, the Rev. Isaac Neville Syer, as Head preferred to live in France!

The Reverend Syer's eldest son, Neville Lord Syer, married the daughter of John Witham of the *Golden Lion*. His eldest daughter, Susan, married the Rev. E. Curteis, curate of Rayleigh in 1823 and afterwards rector of Rettendon. His

81 The Baptist Church in the High Road, which was built in the late 1790s.

second daughter, Georgiana Harriet, married James Byass, a Rayleigh surgeon.

THE BAPTIST CHURCH

The dismissals from the post of rector of Holy Trinity of the Reverends Abraham Caley, John Duffe and John Smith in the 17th century had shown that there were those in the village who favoured a different form of worship from that practised by the established Anglican Church. Over the next 200 years other denominations began to appear, the first of which was the Baptists.

In the summer of 1797 James Pilkington arrived in Rayleigh to spread the word of Baptism throughout the village. His arrival coincided with the mutiny at the Nore, a national crisis focused on a sandbank in the Thames estuary to the south-east of Southend where the English naval fleet frequently anchored, and he had to contend with local unease about any challenge to the accepted order. Rayleigh was said to be rife with drunkenness and unruly behaviour at the time. Nevertheless, Pilkington quickly garnered a core of supporters and was soon struggling to accommodate everyone in the room appointed for Baptist worship. Friends consequently

secured and converted a cart lodge for services which could hold up to 200 people.

Baptism quickly spread and in 1798 James Pearson gave land in the High Road for a purpose-built chapel. The foundation stone was laid on 25 September 1798 and the building opened for worship on 25 March 1799. In 1948, the year the 150th anniversary was celebrated, it was noted that 'the … building is really a wonderful piece of craftsmanship and has thoroughly stood up to the test of time, thus reflecting the greatest credit on the workmanship of those by whom it was erected'.

Pilkington's tenure in Rayleigh was extremely successful and he remained pastor of Rayleigh Baptist Church for over 50 years. He lived in the High Road (on the opposite side, down towards the High Street) and taught local children at his house. He died in 1853 and was buried in the Baptist Chapel grounds.

James Pearson, provider of the land on which the Baptist Chapel was built, was also buried there.

Several other denominations were to follow the Baptists into the village in the following century.

Seven

Nineteenth-Century Rayleigh

❖

By the early 19th century the improved roads were making south-east Essex more accessible to outsiders and guidebooks were being produced to help them understand what they were seeing.

In 1824 *A Guide to Southend* by 'A Gentleman' was published, giving visitors to that fairly new resort information about what to see in Southend and in the surrounding villages. The author wrote somewhat disparagingly of Rayleigh, continuing the trend set by other authors during this period of reduced importance:

'This was once a considerable market town … it is now only an inconsiderable town,

and contains nothing worthy the attention of strangers except the remains of the earthworks of a strongly fortified castle …'

Thomas Wright, whose history of Essex was published in the 1830s, continued the theme of decline, noting that Rayleigh was 'formerly a market town' but that the market had been 'a long-time discontinued'. He was, however, impressed with the church, a 'stately Gothic edifice', and the High Street, from which 'an extensive and interesting prospect is presented over the surrounding country'.

Rayleigh also featured at this time in a guide called *Spas of England*, published in 1841 by Dr A.B. Granville, who visited nearby Hockley spa

82 A rare view of London Hill, up which early 19th-century visitors to Rayleigh usually came.

whilst researching his book. Granville wrote of his journey into south-east Essex that:

> The direct road [to Hockley] is the high turnpike and mail road to Ipswich … as far as Shenfield Lodge, a short distance beyond which it turns to the right, reaching by good turnpike roads, in various turnings and twistings, Wickford, and then Rayleigh; two miles further than which, a little to the left, is Hockley.

Of Rayleigh he wrote that it was 'likely to strike the traveller, even at a distance, from [its] peculiar situation upon elevated ground, commanding various fine prospects all round'. Close-up, he was struck even more by the 'almost startling appearance of green mounds', the motte-and-bailey earthworks of Rayleigh Castle which faced him on his entrance to the village via London Hill.

THE PARISH VESTRY

Administrative affairs in the village were handled at this time by the parish vestry, forerunner of the modern-day town council. This was staffed by the rector and churchwardens of Holy Trinity, the highway surveyors, overseers, rates assessors and the most prominent individuals in the town, i.e. those with substantial landholdings or significant business interests.

Amongst the earliest surviving parish vestry minutes are those from 1778, which record James Fairhead and Samuel Brown as churchwardens and James Blakeley and Edward Burton as overseers. Richard Joslin and Francis Ellis are recorded as parish constables, the local law enforcement officers before the advent of modern policing (see pp.77-8). In these early minutes several vestry attendees signed their name by putting their marks ('X', for example), an indication of the days before compulsory education when not everyone could read or write.

Several names crop up repeatedly in the parish vestry minutes, showing that there was a select band of individuals which was involved in the management of village affairs. The various posts (churchwardens, overseers, surveyors and rates assessors) seem to have been shared around amongst the same individuals.

Most of the earliest discussions revolved around the setting of the rates: how much each individual should be charged as a contribution to parish expenses. Land exchanges, leases, road repairs and the knotty subject of how to care (and pay) for the poor also crop up regularly.

In the 18th and early 19th centuries Rayleigh had a poorhouse or workhouse, which stood in the triangle of land between the High Street and Bellingham Lane. This was established as a result of a charitable donation in 1640 by Isaac Gilbert, who gave property and money towards the schooling of poor Rayleigh children. In about 1730 the two tenements left by Gilbert for this purpose were given up to the parish and used as the parish workhouse.

There are various references in the parish vestry minutes to agreements with individuals to be Governor of the workhouse. For example, on 7 November 1796 the vestry made an agreement with John Pearson of Brentwood that he would run the workhouse and provide meat, drink and clothing for the inmates, plus education in spinning and woollen manufacture. The parish would, for its part, provide funding (an amount per inhabitant), plus furniture, utensils and spinning wheels.

The parish vestry also sought to house local poor people (especially youngsters) with families throughout the village. For example, on 27 April 1810 agreement was reached with Alexander Walford to house Sarah Potter for one year. Walford was given an allowance by the vestry in return. Arrangements of this kind would no doubt have been beneficial all round, with the vestry reducing its expenditure, those housing individuals gaining in income and the individuals themselves learning about family life, increasing in self-esteem and often gaining skills in some kind of trade.

With its responsibility to pay for the poor, the vestry was constantly seeking to reduce the burden on the rates and regularly took action to enforce payments. In 1812 vestry members succeeded in getting William Boyce to agree to 'keep and maintain with all due meat, drink, washing and clothing a female bastard child begotten by him on the body of Sarah Woods, a pauper belonging to the parish'.

Maintaining a rate that was fair to everyone proved difficult. Various individuals, including some on the parish vestry, appealed against the rate that had been set for them. In January 1830 the vestry agreed that the whole rating system should be reviewed as 'it appeared to this meeting highly necessary and expedient that a valuation of all rateable property within the parish should be made to proportion and equalise the rates'. The independent (and consequently impartial) Abraham Offin of Hutton and Charles Matson of Danbury agreed to carry out this review for a sum of £40 each. Correspondence between the vestry and these two individuals reveals that there were approximately 230 dwellings in the parish at this time.

Various prominent individuals in the village feature in the parish vestry minutes.

Amongst these was the Belcham family, whose members had a wide range of business interests throughout Rayleigh, including farming, a draper's, a butcher's and innkeeping at the *Crown*, as well as holding posts such as churchwarden, overseer and surveyor. As with other families in the village, there was a tendency for sons to be named after their fathers – in the Belcham family the name 'George' frequently occurs. In addition, William Belcham was both overseer and churchwarden at different times, whilst Francis Belcham also served as an overseer. W. J. Belcham served as surveyor. William Isaac Belcham lived for a time at Rayleigh House, a prominent building in the High Road.

Unfortunately, the family met with great tragedy in March 1820 when one of the George Belchams (a linen draper) was drowned in the River Thames off Southend when returning with friends from business at Sheerness in Kent. This event affected the entire village. A local newspaper reported that 'every house and shop was closed for business … [and] his funeral was attended by the whole population of the parish'. The Rev. Sir John Head conducted the service and many other clergymen attended.

Arguably the most important individual involved in local affairs in early 19th-century Rayleigh was Thomas Brewitt junior of Down Hall, a wealthy landowner, major employer and long-serving churchwarden in the village. He held the post of surveyor in 1818 and at Christmas 1831 gave 80 stone of beef to the poor.

From the 1830s onwards, the entrepreneur and future Dutch Cottage owner, William Pissey, also began to play a major part in Rayleigh affairs.

ROCHFORD UNION

As time went on and things became more formalised, Rayleigh parish vestry's selections for posts in the village began to have to be ratified by two magistrates. These magistrates met in Rochford, which was increasingly becoming administratively more important than Rayleigh. From *c.*1825 onwards the Rayleigh parish vestry minutes contain signed statements from the magistrates that they accept the nominations made by the vestry and there is increasing evidence of trips to Rochford by vestry representatives.

This subservience to Rochford became much more formalised in 1835 with the advent of what became known as the New Poor Law, following the passing of the Poor Law Amendment Act of 1834.

Before 1835 parishes had been individually responsible for providing for their own poor, usually through the establishment of a parish workhouse supported by funding from the rates. However, this system had been implemented differently in different places; reluctance in each parish to accept a poor person from another parish because of the extra burden on the rates led to disagreements and arguments.

Under the New Poor Law the parishes were stripped of their individual responsibility for poor provision and were instead grouped into Unions, each Union being run by a Board of Guardians. It was the responsibility of the Union to provide a Union Workhouse for all of the parishes which it covered.

In the case of Rayleigh and the other parishes of the old Rochford Hundred, they were all grouped together into a new Rochford Union. A new Union Workhouse was built in Rochford, opening its doors in November 1837. The old parish workhouses went out of use. The one in Rayleigh was sold and demolished.

Rayleigh did not lose complete control, however, since the influential Thomas Brewitt junior was elected first chairman of the Rochford Union Board of Guardians.

Life in the new Union Workhouse was even harder than it had been in the parish one. This was deliberate, for the hard daily grind was designed to discourage idlers and get those who were able to go out to work,

thus reducing the burden on the rates. There was a direct link between the two, as the new Union's Board of Guardians also dictated the parishes' rates.

As time went on the Union's powers increased and those of the parish vestry diminished.

THE CENSUS AND THE TITHE MAP

In 1841 the first national census was taken, being a record of who lived in each house, their ages and, in the cases of most of the adults, their profession or trade. A census has been taken every ten years since then, becoming increasingly sophisticated as time has gone on.

83 The Tithe Map of Rayleigh of 1841. This, and the accompanying Tithe Award on which it was based, together provided the first detailed picture of Rayleigh village, showing all the roads that existed at that time and all the individual properties and who owned them. The familiar pattern of the High Street/Bellingham Lane/Church Street triangle can easily be made out, whilst the circular area to the left is Rayleigh Mount. London Hill, Crown Hill, an embryonic Love Lane (then called Glebe Lane), Hockley Road, Bull Lane, Eastwood Road (Mill Lane) and Castle Road (Meeting Lane) are also clearly visible.

At the same time as the first census was being produced a one-off snapshot was also being taken of who owned (and, where different, occupied) what land in each parish. This was known as the Tithe Award and, in Rayleigh's case, was made in October 1840. The Tithe Award was accompanied by a Tithe Map, based on the Award and produced in Rayleigh's case in 1841.

Thanks to the almost simultaneous production of the census and the Tithe Award/Map a very good picture exists of who lived in Rayleigh in 1840-1 and what property they owned.

When the 19th century opened, the most important individuals in Rayleigh had been land-owning farmers who had inherited the lands of the old Rayleigh manors. Along with the rector and churchwardens, these farmers effectively ran the village, occupying the major positions on the parish vestry and financing improvements. As the century wore on, however, an increasing number of individuals began to set themselves up in business and by the end of the century the balance of power

had shifted from the land-owning farmers to the self-made tradesmen.

The Tithe Award provides evidence of this transition, with the major landholders including both traditionally affluent farmers (such as Thomas Brewitt junior of Down Hall) and up-and-coming entrepreneurs (such as William Pissey). The Belcham family was particularly adept at managing the change, with both farming and retail business interests.

The Tithe Award also includes some major non-resident landowners, such as Sir Thomas Neave (who owned Rayleigh Castle, Kingley Wood, Fisher's Farm and Lubard's Lodge) and John Fane (who owned Great and Little Wheatley).

INTERESTING BUILDINGS

The Tithe Map provides the first large-scale representation of the village centre, giving the names of roads and depicting individual buildings.

The road names throw up a few surprises. Eastwood Road is shown as Mill Lane, Castle

84   Church Street from the windmill. Numbers 4, 6 & 8 Church Street are just visible at the top end of the road.

85 The *Half Moon*, photographed by a well known Essex photographer, Fred Spalding.

Road as Meeting Lane and an embryonic Love Lane as Glebe Lane. Crown Hill has been completed since Chapman and André (1777) and now extends all the way through to the bottom of London Hill.

All the surviving buildings hitherto mentioned are featured. Other significant surviving town centre buildings from this period are nos 4, 6 and 8 Church Street, which bear the inscription 'T.U. 1850'.

As always, public houses were an essential part of village life. William White, author of a *Directory of Essex* in 1848, and Philip Benton both mention five: the *Golden Lion* (known in

86 Rayleigh High Street, *c.*1915, showing on the right the *White Horse Inn*.

87 The *Spread Eagle*, photographed by Fred Spalding.

White's day as the *Red Lion*); the *Crown*; the *Half Moon*; the *White Horse*; and the *Drovers Arms*. These were evidently the five most important pubs in the village centre and from 1811 to 1815 the parish vestry members held

their annual dinner at each of them in turn. All except the *Drovers* were in the High Street. This was on the Hockley Road just before the border with Hockley parish, approximately where Gattens is now. It was so named because it was a popular resting place for sheep and cattle drovers who were taking their livestock to local markets. As it was outside the village centre there were sufficient fields around to provide overnight accommodation for the animals. A collection of newspaper cuttings of Rayleigh, known from a letter found with it as 'Mrs Johnson's Rayleigh Scrapbook', records that on 29 October 1828 an auction of furniture and other household effects took place at the *Drovers Arms*, where George Dowsett had 'disposed of the innkeeping business'.

In 1840 the *Half Moon* was owned by William Wells and occupied by Mary Yell. The *White Horse* was owned by Richard Crabbe and occupied by William Rudkin. The *Golden Lion* was owned by Mary Friend and occupied

88   The High Road, *c.*1915, showing on the left the *Paul Pry*.

by Neville Syer. The *Crown* was owned by George Belcham and occupied by Neville Syer junior.

There were many other pubs in Rayleigh at various times throughout the 19th century. The surviving *Spread Eagle* and *Paul Pry* are both mentioned in the censuses, the latter being named after a meddlesome character in a play by John Poole, a very successful comedy-dramatist in the first half of the 19th century. The play was produced in 1825, though the building which bears its name is considerably older.

Lost pubs include the *Elephant & Castle* (which stood on the corner of the High Road and Castle Road, to which it gave its name), the *Chequers* (which stood on the west side of the High Street and was also known as the *Exchequers*), the *Plough* and the *Bricklayer's Arms*, the latter being out of the town centre in Trenders Avenue off Rawreth Lane.

There was also a brewery and maltings in the village. Claimed benefits for this *c.*1827 were that it was the only one for miles around and that it was close to Leigh-on-Sea for the shipment of materials to and from London. It stood on the west side of the High Street opposite Eastwood Road and in 1840 was owned by Mary Bellingham and occupied by William Cross. Originally called the Anchor Brewery, it was owned in the late 19th and early 20th centuries by Luker's, but ceased production in the 1920s.

One final interesting building of this period is Dollmartons, on the corner of Eastwood Road, which bears the date 1881.

BUSINESS

By the 1840s a whole range of professions had been established in the village: bakers, blacksmiths, brewers, carpenters, coach builders, chemists, coopers, corn merchants, drapers, glovers, greengrocers, hairdressers, land agents, shopkeepers, solicitors, stationers, stay makers, surgeons, vets, watchmakers and many more.

89 The High Street, looking south and showing in the background the cone of Luker's Brewery.

90   An unusual view of the High Street, looking south, with the brewery in the distance (right) and showing some of the businesses, c.1923.

There was a Post Office, run by John Bell, and regular carrier services to London (Thomas & William Pease: Mondays, Thursdays and Fridays) and Chelmsford (John Britton: Tuesdays and Fridays), plus the regular daily coach services to London, Rochford and Southend.

In the 1860s an office of the Post Office savings bank was established in the village, whilst in 1873 there were telegraph facilities.

In 1859 gas was introduced to Rayleigh, with the newly established Rayleigh Gas Company piping it from the gasworks at Southend to its premises in Crown Hill (where the Jehovah's Witnesses Hall now stands). Later, a large gas holder was erected at the bottom of Crown Hill near the railway station. In 1866 William Rose was the gasworks manager. The main public use for gas at this stage was for street lighting. The parish vestry minutes for 28 March 1868 list gas amongst the expenses incurred by the church.

Businessmen of note in the first half of the 19th century included: C.C. Noone, printer of many Rayleigh posters; Joseph Markwell, auctioneer and land agent; and John Witham, coachbuilder. James Rod was auctioneer,

shoemaker, parish clerk and rate collector. John Page was surveyor and John Deely was a postman. By the 1860s Joseph Webster was a prominent butcher.

AGRICULTURE

Although commerce was increasing in the town centre, most Rayleigh people were employed in agriculture, particularly arable farming. Philip Benton noted in the 1880s that 'the pastures surrounding the town are very good, and there is some good and useful land under tillage stretching towards Rayleigh Lodge'.

This heavy reliance on agriculture made Rayleigh susceptible to any decline in farming fortunes and there were several of these in the 19th century. After the Napoleonic Wars the situation was particularly dire and there was a great increase in unemployment. As time went on, increased mechanisation and improved farming techniques only made things worse.

After the passing of the Poor Law Amendment Act in 1834 many agricultural workers chose to seek a better life elsewhere.

In the 1870s there was further depression, caused by a series of bad harvests, a worldwide

91 A country scene, showing agricultural Rayleigh.

slump in wheat prices and competition between UK and foreign farmers. Many struggled to make ends meet and eventually went bankrupt. People left agriculture in their droves. Arable land was left uncultivated and found a use only for grazing.

The future for farming in Rayleigh looked bleak.

RELIGION

At Holy Trinity the rector from 1799 to 1837 was the Rev. Sir John Head. Benton described him as being 'respected by all shades of opinion in this parish', although he was often away, with curates looking after the parish in his absence. He died in 1838.

Head was succeeded by the Rev. Philip Wynne Yorke, rector of South Shoebury,

who held the post until 1843, when he was succeeded by William Twyne.

Twyne was the brother-in-law of the Lord of the Manor of Rayleigh, Robert Bristow. Benton traced the Twyne family back several hundred years, finding one ancestor who was Mayor of Canterbury and another who was mentioned in Camden's *Britannia*.

The Rev. Twyne played an active part in running the parish vestry and also became a magistrate. In 1846 he discovered some chain mail and plate armour in a hole in the chimney at the Rectory. What subsequently happened to this is unclear. He resigned the incumbency in 1871 when 'his health had so far failed as to disable him from officiating in the church'.

Twyne's eldest son Bryan was a captain in the army. His second son, William, unfortunately drowned at the age of just 19 in the River Crouch off Hullbridge during William senior's incumbency at Rayleigh. A tablet on the north wall of the north-east chapel records this tragic event.

One of the churchwardens during Twyne's incumbency was John Page, who died in 1858 and is commemorated by a memorial in the south aisle of the church. His wife, Lydia, who died two years earlier, is similarly commemorated. They lived for many years at Turret House.

The Rev. Twyne was succeeded in 1871 by the aptly-named Joseph Duncan MacVicar. MacVicar and his wife Susan are also commemorated in the church.

In 1873 William Isaac Belcham presented one of the windows in the Alen chapel to the church. The font was also presented at this time, by the Hilliard family, in memory of Mary Meakens Hilliard who died on 13 September 1870.

In 1887 the Rev. MacVicar was succeeded by the Rev. Rolla Charles Meadows Rowse, but continued to be patron for some years afterwards.

James Pilkington's long involvement with the Baptist Church came to an end with his death in 1853. In 1880 another significant local figure in the movement, W.E. Blomfield, was inducted for study. Blomfield went on to become president of the Baptist Union in 1923.

Despite the visit of John Wesley in 1755 (see p.51) it was not until the 1830s that Methodism had a formal presence in Rayleigh. Wesley's colony at Leigh-on-Sea was almost certainly the base from which Methodism spread to Rayleigh and other villages in the Rochford Hundred.

The first documented meetings in the village took place in a house in 1837 in what is now Eastwood Road. However, the catalyst for growth was the arrival in 1842 of Richard and Sarah Frost, glove and straw hat makers respectively from Bury St Edmunds, and, a year later, that of William Blomfield, an insurance agent, linen/woollen draper and tailor from

Ipswich. The Frosts and Blomfield soon realised they shared a common religious view and began to hold meetings in a room over Frost's High Street shop.

Despite this initial interest, the movement did not really get going until 1884 when Samuel Johnson, a grocer from Colchester who had moved to Rayleigh in 1863, made a formal plea to set up a local Methodist Society. A fund-raising campaign was launched and in 1884 a church was erected on land on the corner of the High Road and Love Lane (now the building owned by the Salvation Army). William Blomfield, who was to be 90 years old the following week, took part in the ceremony, but the other founding-father of the movement, Richard Frost, had unfortunately died in 1882.

Another religious movement which arose in the locality at this time was the Peculiar People. This organisation was founded in 1837-8 by James Banyard of Rochford. It took its name from a Biblical quotation meaning that its members had been specifically chosen. Banyard had been inspired to found it following a religious experience in the mid-1830s. He was already a Wesleyan, having been converted to religion after an early life as a drunkard.

This new sect encountered a lot of controversy. The Peculiars professed a belief in divine healing, which meant that when one of their members fell ill they refused to call the doctor, allowing the illness to run its course. This sometimes led to the death of the individual concerned and, when children were involved, there was often an outcry.

In 1855 James Banyard's son fell ill and, fearing that he would die, Banyard called the doctor. This blatant flouting of the rules caused a schism in the movement and Banyard was forced out. He was replaced as leader by Bishop Samuel Harrod, who moved the headquarters from Rochford to Daws Heath. Banyard never regained the leadership and died in 1863.

In 1888 the movement celebrated the 50th anniversary of the conversion of Bishop Harrod. A marquee was erected on a field owned by the Bishop in Mill Lane (Eastwood Road), not too

92   The Wesleyan or Methodist Church (now the Salvation Army Hall), *c.*1915. Love Lane is on the left.

far from his Daws Heath chapel. The Bishop sat on a raised dais, surrounded by church elders and other important figures. He was given 80 gold sovereigns and an illuminated address. Some verses were composed in his honour.

The Peculiar People's first chapel in Rayleigh was in Bellingham Lane. The site is now occupied by the Women's Institute Hall. In 1923 they opened a new chapel in Eastwood Road, now the Evangelical Church.

PUBLIC HEALTH

Although spiritual care was well-established in 19th-century Rayleigh, decent medical care was only now becoming widely available. Health standards and life expectancy were low. The workhouse provided shelter, food, clothing and basic medical attention for the very poorest individuals, but their life was still hard. Most others worked long hours on the land and suffered poor health as a result. Infant mortality rates were high and whole families could be wiped out by an epidemic of some disease.

On occasions, even the village economy could be affected, with the cancellation of the market or the fair due to an outbreak of smallpox or some equally dire disease.

93   The Peculiar People's Chapel in Eastwood Road (now the Evangelical Church). Originally based in Bellingham Lane on the site now occupied by the Women's Institute Hall, the Peculiars moved to Eastwood Road in 1923.

Things were improving all the time, however, and various medical men began to settle in the village and put their knowledge and skills to use.

In 1787 Rayleigh people had been inoculated against smallpox by William Dobson. In 1834 they were offered the choice of inoculation or vaccination (a newer and better form of protection) against another smallpox outbreak. The parish vestry agreed to carry this out free of charge.

The worst fatal disease in the 19th century, however, was cholera. There were several major

94   The graves of James Yell and Dr Hervey Byass, in
the north-west corner of Holy Trinity churchyard.

national outbreaks throughout the century and
in the 1830s at least two people in Rayleigh
died from the disease. Cholera may have been
responsible for the deaths of Susannah Brown,
wife of long-serving parish clerk, Robert
Brown, and James Yell, 44-year-old landlord
of the *Half Moon* inn, whose grave can still
be seen in the north-west corner of Holy
Trinity churchyard.

There was another major national outbreak
of cholera in 1849, when nearby Southend
and Rochford were both badly affected. As
a consequence, the Rayleigh parish vestry set
up a medical sub-committee comprising the
rector, the Rev. Twyne, and the churchwardens,
Thomas Brewitt and John Page, to investigate
health nuisances in the village. Identified
nuisances included open drains, rubbish heaps,
stagnant ditches and stinking privvies. There
was no piped water supply in Rayleigh at the
time – water was taken from ponds, wells and
ditches – and, as it would later be discovered
that cholera was water-borne, this research no
doubt proved invaluable. The pump in the
High Street next to the martyrs' memorial
survives as a reminder of pre-piped water
days.

Perhaps the best-known of Rayleigh's
medical men was Dr Jonas Asplin, a widely-
travelled and well-respected physician who
spent his final years living in the village at

Barringtons (then called Rayleigh Place). Born
in Little Wakering, at the far eastern end of
the Rochford Hundred, he seems first to
have visited Rayleigh in 1826 whilst doing
his rounds. Apart from his medical duties, he
also served from 1834-42 as auditor to the
Rochford Board of Guardians.

Jonas and his wife Elizabeth moved
permanently to Rayleigh in 1839. He died in
1842 and was buried in the churchyard at Holy
Trinity, outside the north-east chapel.

Two other early 19th-century Rayleigh
doctors were William Butler and Hervey
Byass, who operated a local practice together.
Butler purchased the Dutch Cottage in 1811
and evidently owned it until his death in
1859, when it was sold by his executors. Byass
died in 1828 – his grave can still be seen
in the north-west corner of Holy Trinity
churchyard.

The family medical tradition continued
after Byass's death, however, his son James also
becoming a doctor and a medical officer for
the Rochford Union. James lived at Hull Trees
or Holly Trees, formerly known as Rivers, at
the southern end of the village on the High
Road towards the Weir.

Other notable local doctors of the time
included: Charles Carter (who practised
in the 1820s, succeeding William Butler);
George Hilliard (who took on the surgery at
Barringtons (Rayleigh Place) after the death of
Dr Asplin); and Edward Digby (who oversaw
locally the compilation of the 1841 census).
Hilliard and Digby both gave their services to
the Rochford Union. Hilliard also oversaw a
programme of vaccination against smallpox in
the early 1850s.

Another Rayleigh doctor, Robert King,
suffered a great tragedy in the village, with the
death of his wife Sarah (daughter of the vestry
clerk, Joseph Markwell) when she fell from a
horse and cart at the tender age of 23.

Apart from the doctors, shopkeepers were
also playing a role in preventive medicine.
William Pissey, described in several sources as
a chemist and druggist, was at the forefront of
this in 19th-century Rayleigh.

LAW AND ORDER

In addition to the improvements in healthcare which were being made in 19th-century Rayleigh, improvements were also being made to the general protection of people and their property through the advent of full-time policing.

Before 1840 law and order in each parish was the responsibility of the parish vestry, which appointed parish constables to enforce the law. These worked with magistrates, farmers and tradesmen to clamp down on criminal activity. Some judicial matters were also dealt with in the local manorial court for the old Rayleigh manor. The usual venue for these in the late 18th and early 19th centuries was the *Golden Lion*.

Regular crimes handled by Rayleigh's parish constables included theft, drunkenness, assault and moving (especially poverty-stricken) strangers out of the town before they could commit any crimes or become a burden on the rates. Some constables were also tasked with checking that ale measures were upheld in Rayleigh pubs and there was often a parish constable present at Rayleigh Fair. Perks of the job included payment for specific duties and a staff of office which constables could carry whilst on duty.

Many parish constables, however, were inexperienced and untrained and often had other full-time jobs around which to fit their policing activities. In 1843 applicants for the post included blacksmiths, bricklayers, a butcher, a carpenter, a druggist, a plumber and a stationer.

In general, the office was an unpopular one to hold and in Rayleigh's case the parish vestry seems regularly to have appointed the same individuals. William Doe, for example, had several stints in the job, covering 22 different calendar years between 1810 and 1836 inclusive.

The parish constables tended to focus their activity on the village centre, which meant that outlying farms were comparatively unprotected. This was true across the country and in Essex there are many examples of farmers and other property owners banding together to form anti-crime associations to protect their assets.

One such association was in existence in Rayleigh as early as the 1790s. A successor organisation was formed in 1824. It concentrated on rural crimes such as horse stealing and lasted until 1832.

One of the most serious and widely-reported crimes confronting the local parish constables was an arson attack on a barn at Hog Farm, between the High Road and Eastwood Road (then called Mill Lane), roughly in the vicinity of the current police station. This took place, apparently by design, on Guy Fawkes's Night, 5 November 1830.

The event occurred against a backdrop of agricultural unrest throughout the south-east, caused primarily by increased mechanisation (introduced as a result of labour shortages during the Napoleonic Wars) and consequent unemployment. There had already been many cases of rioting, plus arson attacks on agricultural buildings and damage to machinery, most alleged or later proven to have been committed by disgruntled agricultural labourers who had a direct connection with the property in question. Some Essex towns, such as Witham, experienced repeated attacks. In Rayleigh, suspicion fell on one such agricultural labourer, James Ewen.

At the time of the fire, Hog Farm was in the occupation of John Sach, a one-time overseer in the parish. Ewen, who was in Sach's employment, was said to have had a grudge against him, caused by dissatisfaction over low wages and inadequate accommodation.

Witnesses to the fire reported that Ewen had done little to assist with the fire-fighting and had spoken critically of Sach whilst watching the blaze. He was quickly arrested and taken for trial.

Nevertheless, many people remained unconvinced of Ewen's guilt. The two principal witnesses against him were themselves known to be of dubious character, one giving evidence against Ewen to save his own skin and the other allegedly motivated by financial reward, possibly put up by the anti-crime association.

Whatever the truth of the matter, Ewen was convicted of the crime and was hanged at Chelmsford jail on 24 December 1830. His body was returned to Rayleigh, where he was buried in Holy Trinity churchyard.

Several people from outside the village sought clemency for Ewen during the lead up to his execution, but farmers and landowners in Rayleigh seem to have been prepared to accept that he was guilty. Perhaps they felt that his death would serve as an example and a deterrent to others.

Rochford Hundred historian, Philip Benton, claimed that 18 months later a well-known group of arsonists was hanged at Maidstone in Kent and that it was commonly thought that they were the ones who had carried out the attack at Rayleigh.

Full-time police officers (replacing the part-time parish constables) began to appear in Essex with the creation of the county force in 1840, set up as one of the earliest forces in the country following the passing of the 1839 County Police Act. Essex was divided into districts and Rayleigh was made headquarters of a district covering the Rochford Hundred geographical area. There was, however, no official police station in the village at this time and officers operated from their own homes or from rented accommodation. The initial complement in Rayleigh was one superintendent and one constable, out of a total of eight officers in the division.

In 1842 the senior officer was Superintendent Algernon Low, who was thanked that year by parishioners 'for his active conduct during his residence at Rayleigh and for the … manner in which this parish has been in since the established force has been in operation'.

In 1847 a police station was erected in Rochford, then a sub-station to Rayleigh, though the process was underway for these roles to be reversed. The process was completed with the resignation in 1850 of Superintendent Low after ten years' service; Rochford officially replaced Rayleigh shortly afterwards as the divisional headquarters.

In 1855 a restructuring of the county force into nine divisions confirmed Rochford as the headquarters of the local division. Rayleigh officers were still operating from rented accommodation, the top man in the village being Superintendent H. Ackers.

EDUCATION

Improvements were being made, too, in education.

The earliest records of education in Rayleigh are of ad hoc teaching or short-lived charitable provision for a small number of boys, tutored by the Church. The chantry certificate for the Barrington chapel at Holy Trinity (see p.33) included instructions for the chantry priest to teach local children. In 1548 the Chantry Commissioners recorded the existence of a school in Rayleigh, evidently this one. There is also evidence that children were taught in the church porch.

In 1640 Isaac Gilbert donated property and money towards the education of a small number of poor children (Gilbert's property became the parish workhouse – see p.65).

In 1763 the Rev. George Sykes gave £200 to the minister and churchwardens of Holy Trinity for investment, the income therefrom to be used to teach poor children the three Rs. The Rev. Sykes was evidently a socially conscious man, for he gave a further donation of £100 towards feeding the poor.

By the late 18th century, education was becoming more widely available in the village. Sunday schools were becoming more popular and there are many examples of boarding and so-called Dame schools, where children were taught, if the stereotype is to be believed, by an elderly spinster in her own home. In Rayleigh's case there are several instances of husband-and-wife teaching partnerships, usually with the man teaching the boys and the woman teaching the girls. Most schools at this stage were funded by a combination of public subscription, donations from important local individuals and rent from land or property.

The first sign of a purpose-built schoolroom comes in 1792 when the Holy Trinity curate, the Rev. Miles Moor, loaned the churchwardens and overseers £75 'to discharge the expense of building the new schoolroom for the use of the parish'.

This was later replaced by a new building, which is shown on the Tithe Map as a 'Schoolhouse'. It was provided by the Anglican Church and was known as the Church or National School. It was also used as a meeting venue.

The parish vestry also considered the issue of education. In 1844 'it was proposed by the rector [the Rev. Twyne] that a subscription be entered into for the benefit of the parochial schools'. The rector contributed £10, Thomas Brewitt £5 and various other individuals £1 each. It was also resolved that a committee be formed to oversee these finances.

In 1863 the school was demolished and rebuilt, a move financed largely by public subscription. This is the existing building, later the Parish Rooms and most recently Amigo's restaurant. Several additions and alterations were made to it over the next 20 years, including some in 1870, the year stated on the commemorative plaque on the front of the building as the year of its construction. In 1866 John Sparry was teaching the boys and Mrs Bertha Sparry the girls.

95 A well-known engraving of Holy Trinity Church, dating from 1833 and showing the old schoolroom which stood on the site of the now-closed building most recently used as Amigo's restaurant.

The Baptist Church too was active in providing education. The Rev. James Pilkington ran a 'Classical and Commercial Academy' from the earliest years of his ministry which tended to attract the children of non-Anglican parents. A plaque on the wall of Ladbrokes, next to the *Roebuck* public house, records the location of this now-lost building.

This was superseded in 1863-4 by a new building immediately to the north of the Baptist chapel, which became known as the 'British

96 Holy Trinity Church, showing, on the right, the old National School (latterly Amigo's restaurant). This replaced the old schoolroom shown in the previous picture. This photograph was taken after the early 1930s, when Patmore's bakery, which stood in front of the church, was demolished.

97 The British School, built by the Baptist Church for the education of the children of non-Anglican parents in the early 1860s.

School'. Unlike the Anglican National School, this furthered the Baptists' aims of providing non-denominational religious teaching. It attracted people from all over Essex, London and even abroad.

Despite the improvements in formal education in Rayleigh, school attendance was not compulsory and children were often absent. This was usually because they were helping their parents in the fields (especially at harvest time) or attending local events such as the fair. At the National School there was also disruption due to the use of the school in the evening for various social events.

In 1870, however, a new Education Act was passed. This required every parish to have a school and, if no school existed, gave powers to local ratepayers to elect a School Board to raise the money to build one. The School Board could also enforce compulsory attendance.

In Rayleigh, although there were plenty of opportunities for education, the two principal schools, the National and the British, favoured different approaches and were often in conflict. Their differences arose principally from the active teaching of Church of England principles at the National School and of non-denominational teaching at the British School.

Matters reached a head in December 1871 when the British School was closed, largely due to a lack of funds. Some accused the school's

managers of deliberately closing its doors in order to force the creation of a School Board and there was much animosity between the Baptist and National School factions.

A meeting took place on 21 December 1871 'to consider upon and adopt a course which may be thought the most advisable to secure the election of an efficient school board for the parish'. The course decided upon was the creation of a Rayleigh School Board, the first meeting of which was held on 25 January 1872. It was agreed that it would be managed by representatives from both camps to ensure a unified approach.

The National and British Schools were taken over by the Board and became known as 'Board Schools'. The National School became the boys' school and the British School became the girls' and infants' school. John and Sarah Hill were the respective teachers. Infant boys were transferred quarterly to the boys' school.

VILLAGE LIFE

What was there to relieve the drudgery of everyday life in 19th-century Rayleigh?

First there were several royal celebrations.

In September 1831 'the Coronation of their most gracious majesties [William IV and Queen Adelaide] was celebrated here with every demonstration of loyalty'. A quart of beer was given to each of 300 poor people and there was bellringing, band music and the illumination of the streets at night. Newspapers recorded that 'the most cordial good feeling prevailed on this heart-cheering occasion'.

This was followed within the next decade by Queen Victoria's coronation. Later in the century there would be her two jubilees. The Golden Jubilee in June 1887 was celebrated with flags, fireworks and a religious service led by the Reverend William Harding, vicar of Hockley. Rayleigh's rector, the Reverend Joseph MacVicar, hosted a dinner in the boys' (formerly National) school for nearly one hundred over-60s. Children were entertained by a professional conjuror and treated to their own meat tea. A fire was lit on Rayleigh Mount using wood and tar barrels donated by local

98   Rayleigh Fair, probably on what was Webster's Meadow (now the King George Playing Field).

people. A local contractor donated a whole tree for the same purpose. The Rayleigh Drum & Fife Band provided music to accompany the celebrations.

One of the most enthusiastically celebrated events in early 19th-century Rayleigh was the passing of the Reform Bill on 21 June 1832. A marquee was erected in the High Street and a dinner of roast and boiled beef, plum pudding and beer was given to 700 poor people, the food and drink being delivered in two wagons. The event was presided over by the Holy Trinity rector, the Rev. Sir John Head, with assistance from the Baptist minister, James Pilkington.

At 3 o'clock 200 more people were entertained in another marquee. George Belcham chaired the event and toasts were made to the King and the Duke of Sussex. Again there was cannon fire, bellringing and fireworks. Dancing continued to a late hour. The following evening soup was distributed to 126 poor families.

Despite long working hours, residents still managed to fit in time for entertainment.

Chief among the large-scale events was the annual fair (see p.30), but in the latter part of the 19th century there was also a fête, plus occasional wild beasts shows and circuses. The fête, held on butcher Joseph Webster's meadow behind his shop on the east side of the High Street, included such attractions as needlework, a flower show, pony races, fruit and vegetable stalls, bicycle races and fireworks. The fête secretary was Charles Barnard, manager of Luker's brewery.

The inns, pubs and taverns provided on-going entertainment and, along with the Church, were the centre of community life. The *Golden Lion* and the *Crown* also hosted regular meetings of local societies, an increasing number of which were becoming established throughout the 19th century. The school buildings, too, were increasingly popular venues for local society meetings.

Clubs and societies of this era included the Rayleigh Literary & Scientific Institute, the Rochford & Rayleigh Conservative Association, Trinity Masonic Lodge (formed in 1878, with William Pissey as the first 'Worshipful Master'), Rayleigh Dramatic Club, the Dorcas Society (whose female members made clothes for the poor), Rochford Hundred Coursing Club and

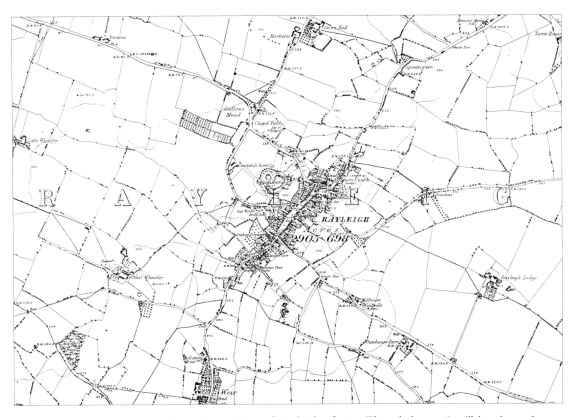

99   The First Edition Ordnance Survey Map of Rayleigh of 1877. The whole area is still largely rural.

a Mutual Improvement Association (whose programme included educational events and music). Other events included Penny Readings and a variety of musical entertainers, such as Signor Jacobowitch from Poland who visited the village in 1834.

Sports in particular were popular. Athletics, cricket and cycling were all attracting participants in Rayleigh in the last decades of the century.

For those who worked on the farm there were regular ploughing matches, with Rayleigh teams competing against representatives from the surrounding parishes. Entrants were judged on the speed and straightness of their ploughing.

FIRST EDITION
ORDNANCE SURVEY MAP

One of the best pictorial representations of late 19th-century Rayleigh is provided by the 1st Edition Ordnance Survey map of 1877.

This shows the built-up village centre, the castle, church and the three surviving windmills, plus the gasworks, the Anchor Brewery and various industrial activities such as brickfields, kilns and blacksmiths.

Outside the village centre, the parish is still predominantly rural, with only a few isolated buildings and farms. Some newer farms have appeared on the landscape, such as Bowdens in Bull Lane and Castlehill Farm at the foot of Crown Hill (then called Crown Lane).

POPULATION

The population of 19th-century Rayleigh reflects this sparseness of development. In 1801 it was a mere 897 people. This had risen to 1,339 by 1831, but the figures remained fairly static from then on, with only slight fluctuations. In 1891 there was even a small decrease to 1,301, 38 fewer than 60 years previously.

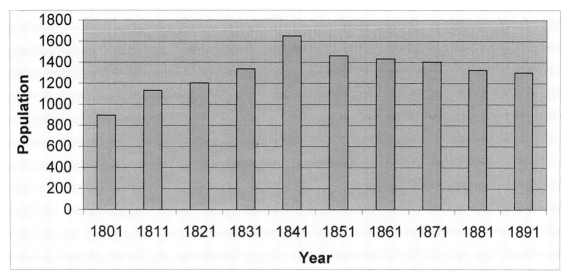

100 A population chart for Rayleigh from 1801 to 1901. The population barely changed during that period, but major growth was just around the corner.

The 1841 figure of 1,651 stands out as a notable exception to this otherwise static trend, but the count for that year was inflated by the taking of the census at the time of the fair.

It would only be in the last decade of the century that the population would begin rapidly to increase.

BARON RAYLEIGH

One individual who deserves a mention at this stage is the 3rd Baron Rayleigh, alias John William Strutt, a noted scientist who discovered argon and won the Nobel Prize for physics.

The Strutt family lived at Terling, near Hatfield Peverel, but took the name 'Rayleigh' for their baronetcy 'because,' according to the 4th Baron, 'it was considered euphonious [i.e. the sound was pleasing to the ear]'. Another theory is that the name was chosen to revive the long-lost but once important medieval baronetcy.

MAJOR CHANGE

Despite the various changes that took place throughout the 19th century, such as new ways of working and new technology, day-to-day life in Rayleigh was still easily traceable back to the medieval period. The population and village layout had barely changed.

Major change, however, was not very far away.

Eight

Transformation

Major change for Rayleigh came in the year 1889 with the arrival of the railway.

Railways made their first appearance in Essex in 1839, with the construction of the main London-Colchester line taking place between 1839 and 1843. This was built by the Eastern Counties railway company, one of the principal railway promoters.

Although this line passed some distance to the west of Rayleigh, it did have its effects on the village. Travellers from London could now take the train to Brentwood and continue their journey into south-east Essex by road. This was quicker and more convenient, and brought with it the novelty of a new mode of transport. Coach companies were quick to recognise the need to embrace the railway and began to time their journeys to meet trains. Goods, including the post, could also be conveyed more quickly.

In 1856 another major line opened in the south of the county, extending from London via the important port of Tilbury to the growing resort of Southend. This line, known as the L.T.S. from the initials of the three towns, was a joint venture between two railway companies, the Eastern Counties and the London & Blackwall. It included a station at South Benfleet, which quickly replaced Brentwood as the preferred local option for Rayleigh passengers. A twice-daily coach service was laid on from the *Crown*. The opening in 1888 of a more direct route between Barking and Pitsea, cutting out the Tilbury 'loop', made journeys to the Capital even quicker.

THE RAILWAY ARRIVES

Several schemes for a railway in Rayleigh were suggested before the final route was chosen. Many of these were for branch lines east from the London-Colchester mainline or north from the LTS. Most were looking for ways to link Rochford to London, but the formidable Rayleigh Hills had to be negotiated and the constructional problems that tunnelling or cutting through them presented put paid to many of the schemes.

In the event, the chosen route went round the Hills to the north. This was the Great Eastern Railway's proposal for a branch line from the main London-Colchester line at Shenfield, calling at Billericay, Wickford, Rayleigh, Hockley, Rochford, Prittlewell and Southend, with a subsidiary branch from Wickford to Southminster. (The Eastern Counties had become part of the Great Eastern Railway in 1862.)

Rayleigh residents welcomed the news enthusiastically. A new line would be good for the transportation of locally-grown produce to London and consequently for local employment prospects.

At a meeting on 17 February 1883 Rayleigh residents and representatives from other parishes were very enthusiastic about the prospect of the railway's arrival. One speaker, Mr R. Henson, speculated that if a station could be provided 'villa after villa would be erected on the hills, and Rayleigh would become a magnificent suburb of Southend'. Another speaker, Mr J. Baker, felt that the railway 'would benefit every place it touched' and that 'if the proposed new railway were made the population of Rayleigh

101 Rayleigh station platforms, *c.*1912. The hill rising up to Rayleigh Mount can be seen on the right.

would considerably increase'. These prophecies were destined to come true.

The line through Rayleigh was officially opened on 1 October 1889. It was initially single track for much of its length, with passing places at Rayleigh station and elsewhere, and was not doubled between Wickford and Rochford until early in the 20th century. There was no public celebration at Rayleigh on the opening day, but 181 people bought tickets and 'the town was alive with excitement'.

On 2 October, 220 Rayleigh children aged from six to 14 were given 3d pieces and buns and taken by train to Southend for a celebratory tea. Another 300 people booked to travel from the town that day.

Initially, not all trains stopped at Rayleigh and the service was somewhat sporadic. Major Rasch, the local MP, took this up with the railway company and improvements were subsequently made. By 1901, with a station,

signal box, goods depot and coal yard all generating employment, there were 30 people working on the railway at Rayleigh.

THE IMPACT OF THE RAILWAY

The arrival of the railway had a huge impact on the village.

Apart from the significant improvement in the speed of travel for residents, there were huge benefits for local businesses. Transportation costs were substantially reduced for Rayleigh farmers who supplied the massive London markets, and many market gardening, orchard and nursery enterprises sprang up as a result.

There was also an influx of outsiders into the village, both in the form of day-trippers coming to appreciate the views and of those seeking permanently to settle in Rayleigh, the latter usually from London.

However, there were also some negative impacts. A whole road transport industry

102 The lower end of Crown Hill (formerly Crown Lane and for a time known as Station Road), *c.*1915, looking towards Rayleigh station. The arrival of the railway in 1889 resulted in Crown Hill replacing London Hill as the main access road to the town centre from the west.

103 Crown Hill, probably in the 1920s, referred to at this time as Station Road and looking towards Rayleigh Mount. The Mount was one of the main features of Rayleigh which attracted tourists coming to the town by railway.

– blacksmiths, carriers, coach builders, horse dealers, ostlers, saddlers, wheelwrights and even publicans – had grown up to support the coach trade. But the arrival of the railway meant that many of these jobs were now redundant.

Furthermore, the road network now needed some adjustment. Hitherto, the main entry into Rayleigh from London had been via London Hill, but the siting of the railway station at the bottom of Crown Hill meant that the latter now provided the most direct route into the village for a growing number of visitors. But Crown Hill was just a dirt track, so it needed making up and widening.

At the top of the hill, the conveniently-placed *Crown* inn benefited enormously from the railway's arrival. Its owner, Frederick Ramuz, a noted local developer and a future mayor of Southend, renamed it the *Crown & Railway* to

cash in on the new trade, purchased the old Rayleigh Castle site for the exclusive use of its visitors and swiftly transformed it into the leading hotel in the town.

Conversely, the *Crown*'s principal rival, the *Golden Lion*, which for a long time had been Rayleigh's leading hostelry but was already in decline, lost out on much of this new trade and fell further into trouble. Its demise was rapid – it lasted just 40 years after the opening of the railway.

Rayleigh landowners quickly came to understand that they possessed a valuable asset. Their land could be sold off at a profit for two principal purposes – the establishment of new market gardens to meet the increased demand for feeding London, and for development to provide housing for the increasing number of incomers.

104 A view back to Crown Hill from Rayleigh Mount, *c.*1925.

105 Rayleigh Mount from the railway station, *c.*1915, with no houses in between. However, the signs of impending development are apparent, with a hoarding from The Land Company advertising freehold plots for sale on easy terms.

106 A view from the tower of Holy Trinity Church, looking east over Fern House, *c.*1915. The surrounding area is still countryside, though development is unfortunately not far off. Note the lack of traffic in Hockley Road.

Later, commuting would begin, sowing the seeds for Rayleigh's evolution into its modern-day role as a commuter town.

DEVELOPMENT

There had been some large-scale sales of land in Rayleigh before the railway's arrival, but after it the Rayleigh landowners acted to sell off their land for development with indecent haste.

In 1890 several small plots in the town centre were put up for sale. In 1891 land to the south of Limehouse Hill was sold off as the Rayleigh Downs Estate.

In 1894 part of a farm called Bowden's in Bull Lane was put up for sale, the land being carefully chosen as it fronted the main (Hockley) road. In the same year the huge Rayleigh Lodge Estate was begun around the old Lodge Farm (formerly the Rayleigh Park hunting lodge) and several new streets – The Chase and Church, Grove, Leslie, Trinity and Warwick Roads – were laid out. Sales of land on White House Farm also took place.

In 1896 land near Rayleigh station in the ownership of *Crown* proprietor Frederick

107 View from Rayleigh Mount, looking north-west and showing London Hill and the railway bridge. London Road can be seen wending its way through the trees behind the bridge and there is one house visible in Down Hall Road (right). Otherwise, the area is completely undeveloped.

Ramuz was put up for sale and a new Rayleigh Station Estate was carved out of former farmland west of Down Hall Road. Streets created as a result included Cheapside, Deepdene Avenue and Eastcheap.

The same year saw the creation of the Limehouse Estate on lands to the north-west

108 Eastwood Road, probably some time around the end of the First World War. Development is creeping eastwards, but at least the roads are still empty.

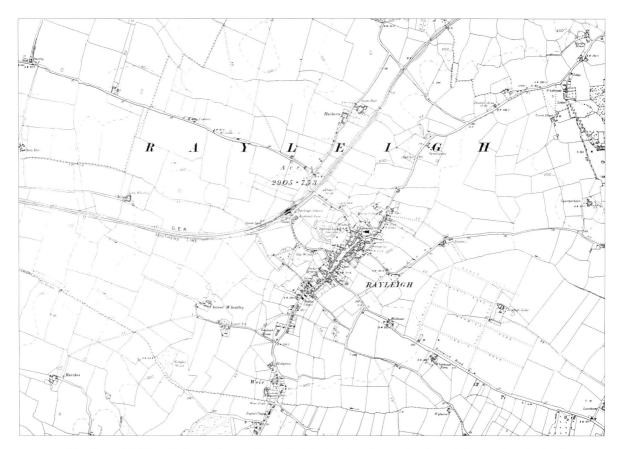

109 The Second Edition Ordnance Survey Map of 1898, showing the curving line of the newly-arrived railway.

of Lime House itself. Clarence, Connaught, Lancaster and York Roads and The Drive were all laid out at this time, whilst eastward extensions of Grove and Warwick Roads were also created.

There followed the Parklands Estate (to the north of Bull Lane, with Alexandra, Louise and Helena Roads being created) and then the Turret House Estate (to the east of Hockley Road, where Wellington, Nelson and Napier Roads were laid out).

Many more developments followed.

Whilst some of the houses in these new roads were bought by local people, many more were sold to outsiders, especially those seeking an escape from London. The population expanded massively during the 1890s and the town became more cosmopolitan as outsiders flowed in.

The creation of these estates opened up many new brickfields in Rayleigh. Hambro brickfield is mentioned in the local authority minutes for 1905, whilst Mr Plowman's brickfield is referred to in 1916. The construction industry consequently provided employment for many Rayleigh people. By 1921 the town's population was over three thousand.

In retrospect, it can be seen, as local historian Noel Beer has recorded, that the railway provided the 'foundation … for the continuing development of the town'.

By 1903 the authors of the first volume of the *Victoria County History* for Essex were already lamenting the changes that had taken place over the previous 14 years.

'With sorrow we have to advise those who wish to see Rayleigh Castle to do so speedily, for the destroyer is at hand; already roads are marked out on the western slope, and soon the grand view will (thanks to modern vandalism) be changed to a prospect of back premises of villas and cottages.'

Unfortunately, things had only just begun.

SECOND EDITION
ORDNANCE SURVEY MAP

The impact of the railway and the development that it initiated are perhaps best illustrated by the 2nd Edition Ordnance Survey Map of 1898. This bears interesting comparison with the 1st Edition map, as there are two immediately apparent differences between them.

First of all, the ugly line of the railway has appeared on the 2nd Edition, its arrival necessitating the diversion of the bottom end of Crown Hill (which for a time would become known as Station Road) and the construction of a bridge over the foot of London Hill. The footpath between the old Great and Little Wheatley manors has been stopped up as a result and the other old manors of Down Hall and Harberts now have the railway line running alongside them. Hambro Hill also now has a railway bridge over it.

The second obvious difference is to the east of the town centre, with the laying out of Church, Grove, Leslie, Trinity and Warwick Roads and The Chase on the lands of the old Rayleigh Lodge as the Rayleigh Lodge Estate. The grid-like nature of this new layout contrasts sharply with the older roads in the parish which had grown up much more naturally, their paths being dictated by local contours and the need for them to lead somewhere rather than dictated by planning.

Expansion is also visible in the town centre, with development having progressed south along the High Road as far as Great Wheatley Road, at the junction with which the imposing Rayleigh House (now 36 High Road) has appeared. Other houses from this period, including some bearing their date of construction, can still be seen on the opposite side of the road today.

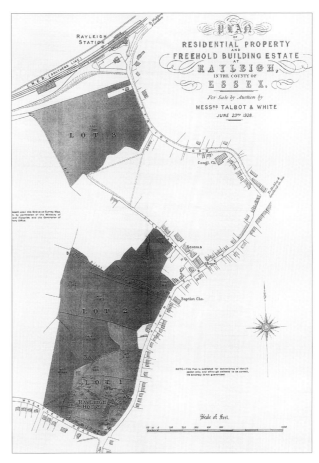

110 The sale plan for the Rayleigh House Estate, showing land to be sold off at auction on 23 June 1928. Advertised benefits for the estate included 'an excellent service of motor buses', 'an elevated and healthy situation', 'a fine range of picturesque panoramic views' and 'a good and abundant supply of water' and gas. It was claimed that the land 'can be advantageously developed as building estates affording many sites for the erection of moderate size residences which are in great and increasing demand'.

THE COUNTY, DISTRICT
AND PARISH COUNCILS

The railway and the widespread development it initiated were not the only major changes to affect Rayleigh at this time. There were changes too in the management of the fledgling town.

In 1889 a new county-wide authority was created – Essex County Council. The effects of this were felt almost immediately, with the parish vestry minutes of 23 July 1889 recording that the County Council had requested a list 'of all properties in this Parish liable to be assessed towards the County Rate'. The Parish sent in a financial return in reply.

In 1894 there were further changes. Under the Local Government Act of that year, district and parish councils were created. The old Rochford Union was replaced by a new Rochford Rural District Council and the Rayleigh parish vestry was replaced by a new Rayleigh Parish Council. There were therefore now three levels of local authority – Parish, District and County.

The parish council met for the first time on 17 December 1894. The meeting was held at the boys' school (the old National School). Mr S. S. Baker was elected chairman (an office he held until April 1899) and the others present were Messrs C. Byford, James Findlay, William Fox, Samuel Gilson, C. Harvey, Hawken, T.W. Offin, the Rev. R.C.M. Rouse and White. C.E. Judd, assistant overseer, was appointed parish clerk. Councillor Baker went on to become chairman of Rochford Rural District Council in 1908. The town's first female councillor, Mrs Frances Cottee, was elected in 1925.

The first item of parish business was to ascertain whether or not there was any interest from local people in having allotments. There was not.

Other items with which the Council had to deal during its early years included: the maintenance of (gas-supplied) public street lighting and the provision of additional lamps; the making up of roads and pavements; and the taking of action against building encroachment onto public roads.

One of the first major decisions made by the Council was the abolition of Rayleigh fair (see p.30). As early as November 1895 the Council resolved 'to convene a parish meeting for the purpose of discussing the advisability of having this fair abolished'. Local residents proved sympathetic and in January 1896 the Council wrote to the Rural District Council formally to request the fair's abolition. James Rogers, the lord of the manor, agreed to surrender fair and market tolls in return for compensation of £25

and on 8 August 1899 the fair was formally abolished by order of the Home Secretary.

WATER SUPPLY

The Council was also active early on in trying to improve the growing town's infrastructure. With gas already sorted, the first priority was the provision of a piped water supply (instead of wells and ditches).

As a first step, a committee was convened in March 1895 'to examine the water supply on London Hill', but progress was to be painfully slow and over the next four years the Parish and Rural District Councils spent much time trying to determine the best way forward for the parish.

In 1898 the District Council announced that it was considering introducing a water supply scheme for the western part of the District, including Rayleigh. Local residents were in favour on condition that the County Council would meet the expense and not increase the rates to fund it. This was to be the first of many decisions where residents and/or the Parish Council put finance ahead of comfort.

Nevertheless, the matter rumbled on and the scheme was not implemented until after 1905. Even then, residents were unhappy with the cost and in 1911 the Parish Council asked the District Council to sell its water undertaking to the Southend Waterworks Company, which it felt would be able to provide water at a cheaper rate. The District Council agreed and eventually the water undertaking was transferred.

As time went on more and more water mains were provided, with ditches being filled in and underground pipes being laid ever more widely across the parish.

The pump in the High Street opposite Crown Hill survives as a reminder of the days before piped water.

SEWERAGE

The related topic of sewerage provision was also addressed from an early date, but this was to take even longer to resolve.

The situation was evidently dire. In January 1895 it was resolved 'that the District Council

III Flooding in Rayleigh High Street, 1910. Surprisingly for a town on a hilltop, flooding was a regular occurrence in Rayleigh. The problem was not resolved until a piped drainage scheme was introduced to replace the overloaded ditches.

be called on to abate the nuisance on the south side of Love Lane caused by the discharge of sewage matter into a ditch'.

Nine months later there were cases of diphtheria in the parish. The District Council's Medical Officer reported that Rayleigh's drainage was 'very defective' and a committee was set up to investigate putting in sewers, the intention being to discharge them from the High Street down Crown Hill. A subsequent inspection revealed that open barrel drains were discharging into Crown Hill, London Hill and Bull Lane. The committee recommended improved drainage and ventilation shafts.

There were still problems, however, 11 years later when in October 1906 it was reported that

a ditch in Bull Lane was causing a nuisance. It was agreed that it should be piped.

In May 1907, Councillor W.H. Rand, who had been elected only the previous month, proposed as one of his first contributions the construction of a parish-wide sewerage scheme. Astonishingly, his proposal received no seconder and consequently further complaints followed.

It took until June 1912 for any positive, co-ordinated action to be taken, when the District Council wrote advising that it was planning to introduce a sewerage scheme for the parish. The Parish Council responded by seeking the views of other Parish Councils within the District Council's area (Thundersley, Hadleigh,

112   Rayleigh High Street, *c*.1915.

etc.). It concluded from the feedback (not surprisingly given its views on the water supply scheme), that the District Council's proposed costs were too high. It did acknowledge that the provision of more sewers would be beneficial, but its official reply, in October 1912, was that councillors did not consider that the Parish was sufficiently developed yet to warrant the extensive scheme being proposed.

Costs and wrangling between the parishes and the District Council were to delay implementation for another decade.

THE ROADS

Another issue which came increasingly to occupy the Council's time was traffic.

As early as December 1896 'the clerk was directed to draw the attention of the County Council to the narrow and dangerous state of the road at the entrance to the street between the *Half Moon* inn and the shop and premises occupied by Mr W. Smith as the road in question is greatly used by the

inhabitants'. Many similar complaints followed and it became something of a policy to try to persuade local landowners to sell off parts of their land to permit road widening at the most dangerous points.

One of the most dangerous bends was in Eastwood Road at Picton House (built on the site of the windmills and now occupied by Picton Gardens), first mentioned as a problem in April 1904. There were several accidents at the site and it became the subject of regular correspondence between the various local authorities. In April 1905 Councillor W.H. Clark, District Councillor for Rayleigh, attended a Parish Council meeting to hear about the 'exceedingly dangerous condition of the road in Mill Lane [Eastwood Road] … which is of insufficient width for one car to pass another with safety and foot passengers are in danger of being run down'.

By July 1909 traffic in the town centre had increased so much that it was 'resolved that Superintendent Pryke be asked to retain the services of both the sergeant and the constable on Bank Holidays and the Sunday preceding for the purpose of regulating the traffic at the Crown Corner and Eastwood Road'.

Another early problem was Bellingham Lane, described in 1914 as 'practically a death trap, the road being so narrow'.

Also in 1914 the County Council advised that it was planning to widen Crown Hill, due to the increase in traffic there.

The Parish Council also oversaw the making up of roads and footpaths throughout the parish. For example, in January 1902 councillors asked the District Council 'to make up the road known as Love Lane and continue the footpath from the Infants' School to the stile leading to the station'. In November 1905 councillors received a petition from Castle Road residents complaining about the bad state of their road.

The Council also took steps to improve the street scene. In September 1903 it accepted an offer from Edward Francis for planting 12 trees in the High Street. Some of these still survive.

THE FIRE BRIGADE

In 1904 the Parish Council decided that it would be a good idea to introduce fire-fighting provision for Rayleigh. Within two years it had purchased two 60-feet lengths of hose and associated equipment and it continued to add to this inventory over the coming years. The question of purchasing a fire engine, which would incur larger costs, was deferred for the time being, though the Council did make enquiries of other local authorities to see how they handled fires.

The Council eventually sought tenders for a fire truck (basically a handcart on which all the equipment could be carried) in 1907. The contract was awarded to the local coach builder, H. Witham, and it was agreed that the truck and equipment should be stored in W.E. Smith's shed in Eastwood Road.

In 1908 the Council established a fire brigade committee and one of its earliest decisions was that an official fire brigade should be formed. This appears to have taken place by

July 1909 under the guidance of ex-sergeant Gentry, though arrangements must still have been informal since in 1917 the Council was still considering 'the question of the formation of a Fire Brigade'.

In 1909 the Council wrote to the District Council asking for the latter to finance the purchase of a fire engine and four years later it wrote to both Southend Borough and Leigh Urban District Councils, requesting the assistance of their brigades in the event of a conflagration in Rayleigh.

LIGHTING

In 1907 responsibility for street lighting was formally handed over from the District to the Parish Council. The latter established a lighting committee to deal with it and set about providing new lamps at strategic locations. Two of the first to be put up were in Eastwood Road, in the vicinity of the dangerous Picton House Corner.

Over the next two decades streetlamps were provided more widely throughout the growing town.

BUSINESS

With a growing population to serve, Rayleigh's businesses prospered. There was a Post Office, a bank (Barclay & Company) and a whole range of tradespeople.

In the first decade of the 20th century principal businessmen included: William Chippington (a coach builder); George Dawson (chemist, druggist and photographer); James Devenish (coal merchant); Percy Deveson (draper); Charles Gainsford Dixon (clothier and draper); Thomas William Finch (ironmonger); the Gilson Brothers (grocers); Samuel Gilson (insurance agent); Henry Mann & Sons (grocers); William Henry Rand & Sons (nurseryman); Ernest Percy Rand (nurseryman); Arthur James Upson (saddler and harnessmaker); Joseph Webster (butcher); and Horace Witham (wheelwright). There was also a healthy population of businesswomen, including: Miss May Dixon, who ran a fancy repository; and Miss E.B. Curnock, a stationer.

With development prospering the Down Hall Brick Company was doing good business, whilst the many builders included J.T. Byford & Sons, who would go on to build many properties throughout the town.

In 1913 Rayleigh gasworks was taken over by the Grays & Tilbury Gas Company. This was a much larger concern, with operations stretching south-westwards as far as Rainham. This gave the town access to a larger and more resolute gas network.

Also by 1913 a telephone exchange had opened in Rayleigh. This was situated at Ernest Patmore's bakery, a building demolished in the 1930s and also known as Wisteria House which stood in front of Holy Trinity Church, facing the High Street.

RELIGION
At Holy Trinity the task of administering to the railway-age flock fell to the Rev. Rolla Charles Meadows Rouse, who succeeded the Rev. MacVicar as rector in 1887 and served on the Parish Council. The Rev. Rouse was also incumbent when two new bells were

113   George Dawson, a pioneering photographer who took many early photographs of Rayleigh, pictured c.1901.

114   The premises of Witham's, 'carriage builder' and 'funeral furnisher', c.1909.

added to the existing ring of six in 1898 to commemorate Queen Victoria's Diamond Jubilee the previous year.

He died in 1904 and was succeeded by one of Rayleigh's most significant modern-day rectors, the Reverend A. Girdlestone Fryer. In 1908 the Rev. Fryer wrote a book called *Rayleigh in Past Days*, which was targeted at the many new settlers in the town who wanted to know something about Rayleigh's history. He also took early steps to protect the town's heritage, overseeing a major restoration of the church between 1912 and 1914. In 1932 he wrote a second book called *Rayleigh Yesterday & Today*, outlining the changes that had taken place in the town during his incumbency.

At the Methodist Church the movement continued to expand. In 1902 a new Sunday school building was erected next to the church on the corner of the High Road and Love Lane.

In 1904 the Rev. Nehemiah Curnock took over as minister, arriving in Rayleigh from nearby Southend. Already the son of a Wesleyan minister, he went on to become one of the movement's most notable local figures, editing the journal of John Wesley and helping with the production of Methodist hymnbooks.

The Rev. Curnock's daughter, Ruth, was also active in the town, in support of the suffragette movement. It is said that the smashing in 1911 of the window of the old Post Office was carried out by her in the name of this cause.

At the Peculiar People's chapel there were also changes. In 1891 Bishop Samuel Harrod was forced out following allegations about his association with a married woman in the congregation. Most of his flock deserted Daws Heath and he went to preach in a room over a shop in Rayleigh.

He was replaced by Daniel Tansley, though a strong body of anti-Tansley supporters sought for a time to reinstitute Harrod as leader and built their own new chapels near to the original ones.

The deaths of Tansley in 1897 and Harrod in 1898 broke the organisation up into a number of factions until in 1913 the different groups were reunited.

A new chapel was opened in Eastwood Road, Rayleigh in 1923, replacing the one in Bellingham Lane, which was subsequently taken over by the Salvation Army.

In 1956 the Peculiar People joined the Union of Independent Evangelical Churches.

At the Baptist Church in 1893 members were treated to a sermon by Arthur T. Upson, who went on to serve as a missionary in North Africa and to found the Nile Mission Press. He lived in Rayleigh, above a shop on the site now occupied by Stevens' jewellers.

A difference of opinion was, however, bubbling in the Baptist congregation and *c.*1897 a split occurred. The then minister, the Rev. W. J. May, left the movement, taking a number of supporters with him, to found the Rayleigh Tabernacle on Crown Hill (then called Crown Lane).

This was the building now occupied by the United Reformed Church. The site on which it was built had been purchased in 1898 by a Benfleet builder, Edward Watts, for the specific purpose of building a church. Mr Watts proved to be a generous man, paying for much of its construction himself. A memorial brass was erected there in his memory in 1923.

The Rev. May was invited to lead the ceremony for the laying of the foundation stones. A small crowd gathered to hear that this would be a Baptist Tabernacle, though open to worshippers from other denominations.

Six foundation stones were laid by Messrs Watts, May and Ramsey and Mrs Groom, Mrs Houghton and Mrs Abel. A tea was held afterwards and a public meeting followed in the evening. The building was formally opened in July 1899.

After the initial impetus, the Tabernacle movement suffered some difficulties, especially financial ones. By 1909 money was so tight that the building was rented out to help with its upkeep. This drastic move brought forth new life, however, as it was rented for three months by a London minister, the Reverend J. Westbury Jones, who used it to advertise his plans to form a new Congregational Church in Rayleigh.

115   Rayleigh Congregational Church, a building originally constructed as The Tabernacle, the meeting place of a breakaway faction of Baptists. It is now the United Reformed Church.

The Congregational movement in the town was traceable back to Abraham Caley in the 17th century (see p.46) and the Rev. Jones' appeal was met positively by local people. On 15 December 1909, 23 members signed up, several coming from the now-defunct Tabernacle movement.

Once again the generosity of Mr Watts came to the fore. He turned down a handsome offer for a non-religious use of his former Tabernacle building and sold it to the Congregationalists in 1910 on very generous terms.

The Church was formally inaugurated in June 1910 and in October of that year the Rev. George Butcher of Shoreham became its first minister.

Membership increased rapidly, with various members of the Hall family being prominent. Mr Edward G. Hall transferred from Rochford's Congregational Church in August 1911 and Mr H.C. Hall joined in February 1912. The latter was still a member at the Church's 50th anniversary celebrations in 1960! Another member, Mr A.G. Greenhalgh, worshipped at the church for nearly 40 years until his death in 1951.

In 1913 the Rev. Butcher was succeeded by Reverend Thomas W. Mason, whose 13-year ministry was marked by several significant achievements, notably the construction of the adjacent Caley Memorial Hall, named in memory of the one-time non-conformist Holy Trinity rector. The stone-laying ceremony took place on 22 July 1914, with one stone being laid on behalf of Dr Joseph Caley of Philadelphia, a descendant of the Rayleigh rector, by Mrs Charlotte Skinner, mother-in-law of the Rev. Mason and author of a book about Caley.

The Rev. Mason wrote a Pageant on Rayleigh's history in 1925 and also served on the parish council. He resigned in 1926 due to ill health. His successor, Hector MacDonald, was inducted in 1928.

EDUCATION

With the increasing population the still comparatively new schooling provision was already becoming inadequate. Consequently, in May 1895 a new Council School was opened in Love Lane and the infants moved out of the

116   Rayleigh Infants' School, *c*.1906-7.

117   Rayleigh Girls' School, *c*.1910.

girls' (former British) school into the new premises. The new building was designed to cater for 72 infant pupils of both sexes but by 1899, under headmistress Miss Isabella Hyatt, it was averaging an attendance of 80 pupils.

In 1902 a new Education Act abolished School Boards and gave responsibility to the local education authority, in this case the Rural District Council.

The new controlling authority was swift to act. In 1904 the nine-year-old Love Lane infants school was extended and the junior boys moved onto the site as well. The old boys' (former National) school building was no longer required and reverted to church use as the Parish Rooms. Parish Council meetings were also transferred to the new school.

118   An entry at Rayleigh carnival in 1908, a popular event with Rayleigh schoolchildren.

119 The King's Royal Rifles on parade in Rayleigh High Street in 1915. This was one of several military groups to be based in the town in the early years of the First World War.

In 1906 the Rural District Council proposed the erection of a new girls' school, as the girls were still making do with the former British School's cramped premises. However, the Parish Council was against this, resolving to draw up a petition opposing its construction on the grounds that it was 'unnecessary'. No doubt they had the potential cost in mind.

Nevertheless, a third new building was soon erected on the Love Lane site, opening in 1909. The boys moved into it and the girls transferred to the (1904) boys' school in Love Lane. The old girls' (former British) school became surplus to requirements. Boys, girls and infants were all now based in Love Lane.

THE FIRST WORLD WAR

The coming of the First World War in 1914 focused attention on national events, but there were still local implications.

This is best summed up by an entry in the Parish Council minutes in April 1915, almost certainly written by the parish clerk, Charles Ernest Judd:

'The Great War of 1914 commenced August 4, is still raging fiercely and many of the inhabitants have joined His Majesty's forces. A volunteer corps has been raised from the inhabitants of Rayleigh numbering some 120 for home defence. Raids by hostile aircraft are of frequent occurrence and to minimise the damage from incendiary and explosive bombs

120   Rayleigh men who served in the First World War.

lights are extinguished and the town at night kept practically in darkness.'

The 16th King's Royal Rifles, the 18th Middlesex, the 2/1st Cambridgeshire, the 4th Essex, the 2/4th Suffolk, the 1/8th Essex Cyclist Company and the West Somerset Yeomanry were all successively billeted in the town in 1915 and 1916. Many of the soldiers were newly enlisted, training in the town before being posted to the Front. They stayed with local residents, sometimes four or five soldiers per house and usually only for a few weeks.

Sunday services for the men were sometimes conducted on the north slope of Rayleigh Mount and they used the Parish Rooms (formerly the National School) as a club room. They also occupied the old British School at the Baptist Church and a canteen was opened in the town to serve them.

In June 1915 the Parish Council wrote to the District Council to ask that 'the terms of the scavenging contract [essentially cesspool emptying and associated refuse collection] are strictly adhered to, owing to the large number of soldiers now billeted in the place'. In October they approached the County Council to ask

for kerbs to be whitened, to assist night-time travellers during blackout. In December the daily evening post delivery was discontinued due to the 'National Crisis'.

From 1915 onwards the Germans began to launch zeppelin raids on England. Later, aeroplanes were used. The Reverend Fryer, who saw a famous Essex zeppelin crash at Billericay from the windows of Rayleigh rectory, recalled that 'many may remember how one night 19 bombs were thus dropped and exploded in the near neighbourhood of Rayleigh houses'.

Writing in 1932 of these attacks, the Reverend Fryer, often a prophet, reflected that 'this new

121   Rayleigh football team, 1919-20.

horror in warfare … arouses terribly distressing thoughts … as one realises that in a future war this sacrifice of civilian life will be vastly increased, as science is continually discovering new methods of destroying human lives …'.

Towards the end of the war, food production was increasingly important and in April 1917 the District Council wrote to the Parish Council 'asking for particulars of any unoccupied land suitable for cultivation'. The following year the Council, the Rayleigh Food Producers Association and a landowner, Mr Finch, reached agreement on the provision of allotments on Mr Finch's land in Eastwood Road.

In April 1918 the Rev. (later Councillor) Thomas Mason of the Congregational Church wrote to the Council 'calling attention to the fact that the more nervous inhabitants of Rayleigh had remained in a needlessly prolonged state of suspense through not hearing the 'all clear' signal at Southend [after air raids]'. The Council agreed that one of the buglers of the Boys' Life Brigade would sound the signal locally as well.

Several memorials of the First World War survive in the town. In Holy Trinity Church the screen between the south aisle and the Alen Chapel is dedicated to the memory of Reginald Chapman, who was killed on active service. His grave, and those of other soldiers who died in the conflict, can be seen at the cemetery in Hockley Road. Also in Holy Trinity, the east window, put in in 1921, is a memorial of the conflict, whilst a list of those killed during the War can also be seen in the church and on the wall of the neighbouring Royal British Legion Hall. The Rayleigh branch of the Legion was formed by ex-servicemen in March 1923.

Peace celebrations took place on 19 July 1919. They included religious services, and free teas and activities for children and the elderly in a field off Bull Lane. The Parish Council chairman, Mr C.J. Barnard, was presented with a machine gun by the War Office as a memento of the war, but this was later broken up for scrap.

The Reverend Fryer later wrote that 'it must be said of the people of Rayleigh that they showed throughout these war days a calmness and a readiness to sacrifice and endure of no mean order'.

THE CEMETERY

By the early 1880s the churchyard at Holy Trinity had become full and a new cemetery had been opened outside the town centre in Hockley Road.

With the advent of the parish and district councils, control of the cemetery had passed to the Rural District Council. In 1907 the Parish Council wrote to the District Council, asking if they could take control of it. However, such was the legality surrounding the transfer that it was to be the late 1920s before it actually took place. In the interim, the District Council did allow the Parish Council to have an input into their decisions. One of the main ones was to increase its size – essential following the increase in population.

By January 1924 expansion of the cemetery was considered 'most urgent' and the Council began to negotiate with local landowners regarding the purchase of an adjacent field. However, residents living nearby objected and negotiations dragged on for a few more years.

Control of the cemetery officially passed from the Rural District Council to the Parish Council on 1 October 1924, though some of the more complicated legal points took a bit longer still to resolve.

Eventually, in 1928, the Parish Council managed to secure a field next to the existing cemetery, more than doubling it in size.

COUNCIL HOUSES

The increasing population drew attention after the war to the inadequacy of some of the residential properties in the town.

As early as June 1914 the Council had received a letter from Mr W.H. Rand asking them to consider the provision of 'workmen's dwellings' (Council houses) in the town. No action was taken and in December the Council actually voted against providing any such houses.

The subject was picked up again in the early 1920s when the Council was more receptive to the idea. Councillors sought financial assistance from the government, but the Minister of Housing wrote in 1924 to say that this would not be forthcoming because 'in his opinion the need does not arise, owing to the large amount of building now going on'.

Despite this, the Council pressed on with its plans and in 1926 began to invite applications from residents who wished to live in the proposed new properties. Forty-three applications were received and the Council decided that the first two houses would be allocated to George Garwood and Joseph Little. The first such houses, now just weeks away from construction in Hambro Hill, were to be called 'Hambro Cottages'.

These were to be the first of many Council houses. In 1927 more were approved in Daws Heath Road.

THIRD EDITION
ORDNANCE SURVEY MAP

In 1923 the 3rd Edition Ordnance Survey Map for Rayleigh was produced. This shows continued development, particularly in the east around Rayleigh Lodge and to the north-east around Victoria Road. Jubilee and Louise Roads link the two estates via Bull Lane.

Other items of interest are the numerous nurseries which have grown up following the land sales in the 1890s and the brickworks which have been created to meet the demand for new houses. The cemetery, soon to be extended, can also be seen.

TRAFFIC

The thorny problem of increasing traffic continued to make itself felt in the High Street, both from through-traffic and from the increasing numbers of visitors who were coming to Rayleigh for a day out.

In 1919 'the clerk was instructed to write to Superintendent Perry, calling attention to the danger which children are subject to when begging from passengers in the large motor

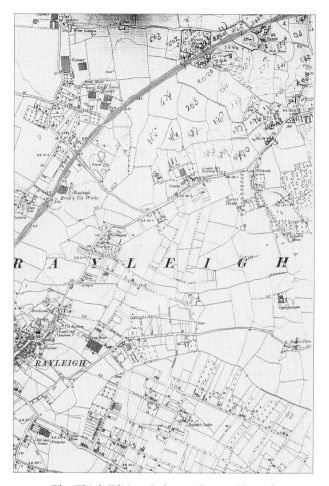

122 The Third Edition Ordnance Survey Map of 1923, showing the north-eastern area of the town.

vehicles which frequently visit Rayleigh during the summer season'.

Two years later the Council wrote to the Essex Chief Constable to ask for an extra police officer and to point out 'the need for a man to be on point duty almost constantly at the Eastwood Road corner due to the daily increasing traffic'. The situation had still not resolved itself by 1925, so in July the Council decided to seek the demolition of properties on the corner of Eastwood Road and High Street to improve traffic flow at the junction. Similar improvements were made at the junction of the High Street and Crown Hill.

In 1922 the Rayleigh Ratepayers Association wrote to the Council to ask for a speed limit in

123   Rayleigh High Street, probably in the 1920s.

the main road. However, the Council concluded that this was 'not considered desirable' for the time being.

PUBLIC TRANSPORT

On 1 January 1923 a nationwide reorganisation of the railway network took place and the GER became part of the London & North Eastern Railway (LNER).

By this stage another form of public transport, the motorised omnibus, had appeared on the scene.

As early as 1906 the Southend & District Motor Bus Company had begun running services from Southend to Rayleigh, but opposition from Southend Corporation and competition with the railways meant that the scheme foundered after only a few months. Over the next 20 years many other companies set up in business.

In 1914 one of the most successful, the Westcliff-on-Sea Motor Charabanc Company Limited, started operations in the Southend area. By 1921 it had evolved into Westcliff Motor Services (W. M. S.) Limited and started running services to some of the outlying towns, including Rayleigh. A period of steady expansion followed and over the years W.M.S.

was to become one of the largest and best-known bus companies in the area.

Another major player was the Eastwood-based Bridge family, whose Edwards Hall Motors company sought to open up new routes for passengers who lived in areas not served by Westcliff.

The Bridge family had taken its company's name from Edwards Hall in Eastwood (owned by Henry Ritchie Bridge) and was responsible for developing some of the land there near Eastwood Rise and Tudor Road. Building was actually the family's principal business, but their Eastwood estate was badly situated for public transport, so they decided to set up their own company.

Bus transport as a whole continued to improve throughout the 1920s as bus services became more frequent and cheaper. There was even a Rayleigh & District company for a while. The Parish Council minutes of October 1921 record that there were 'motor buses plying for hire' regularly in the High Street.

This brought with it a whole range of problems, however, including such things as 'the overhanging trees on the line of route taken by the motor buses between Rayleigh and Southend-on-Sea, which trees are dangerous to outside passengers'.

In 1929 the Parish Council wrote to the County Council to ask for the railway bridge at the bottom of London Hill to be widened 'in view of the increasing number of buses, charabancs and motor traffic generally' that was passing underneath it. The County Council replied that it would be too costly to widen the bridge and in any case the Rural District Council 'have included in their Town Planning Scheme a bypass road from the *Carpenter's Arms* [in neighbouring Rawreth parish] to the new Arterial Road [see below], which improvement when effected would relieve the bridge of a large portion of the traffic'. The Parish Council replied that 'traffic which renders the bridge most dangerous consists principally of buses and motors, such traffic increasing daily, and will not be lessened even when the suggested bypass road is completed'. Matters were at a

124 The new junction at Rayleigh Weir in 1928, shortly after it opened. The view is looking north towards Rayleigh. The Arterial Road crossed the old Rayleigh-Thundersley road to create this new, important junction. The man in the photograph is probably an AA patrolman, as there was regularly one on duty there in the first few years following the opening of the new road.

stalemate and it would be another 35 years before the bypass was built.

THE SOUTHEND ARTERIAL ROAD

By the early 1920s, as intimated above, things were also happening on the wider travel scene.

The volume of traffic coming into south-east Essex, and particularly to nearby Southend, was such that a major new road was required to cope with it. The route chosen was along the southern boundary of Rayleigh parish and the road, the Southend Arterial Road (now the A127), was duly constructed and officially opened at Southend on 25 March 1925. Its construction required the fencing off of the weir and pond near Weir Farm, Rayleigh, to improve safety.

The arrival of the new road was a significant point in Rayleigh's transport history. For the first time, the gateway to the Hundred moved from Rayleigh High Street and the new gateway, known as Rayleigh Weir, quickly became a very busy junction.

As early as September 1925 the Parish Council wrote to the Essex Chief Constable to 'call attention to the fact that the new London

Road cuts through at right angles the Hadleigh to Rayleigh Road causing a most dangerous spot near the weir. An AA man is constantly on duty here ... but he has not the influence that a constable has over traffic'.

A new *Weir Hotel* opened at the junction to serve the passing trade. In 1929 the proprietor was Mr A.W. White.

EMERGENCY SERVICES

In 1912 there had been a proposal for the establishment of a hospital in the town. Doctor Egleston Burrows of Rayleigh House, a large imposing property on the High Road towards the Weir, had 'expressed his willingness to give a site for, and defray half the cost of building, a hospital and provide half the necessary equipment'. Nothing came of this, however, no doubt because of the advent of war.

By 1920 the subject of emergency medical care arose again and in February that year Ernest Percy Rand, nurseryman, parish councillor, future Parish Council chairman and someone who would go on to give many years' public service to the town, 'reported that a motor ambulance had been placed under his control

125 A later photograph of Rayleigh Weir, *c.*1950, now with a more familiar look to it. The licence for the *Weir Hotel* was transferred from the *Elephant & Castle*.

… [and that he had] secured the services of Mr W. Pudney as driver'.

Two years later Mr Rand, who lived for a time at Picton House, was active in a related sphere, reporting that a Volunteer Fire Brigade had been formed. In 1923 Harry Smith was Fire Brigade captain, responsible for drill and training.

In 1926 the Council secured a loan from the Ministry of Housing for the purchase of a motor fire pump from the Simonis company, moving up from the old horse-drawn handcart of pre-war days. The engine cost just over £692. The words 'Rayleigh Parish Council' were to be etched on the side and Mr Jarvis agreed to store it on his premises.

One disappointment was that the construction of a fire station was excluded from the loan because the Ministry felt that it would 'have the effect of diverting skilled building labour from the erection of houses'.

The parish councils at Rawreth, Hockley and Hawkwell all offered to pay towards the cost of the brigade in return for their parishes being covered.

The arrival of the Arterial Road led the local police to relocate from the town centre to the Weir, a move which proved unpopular with Rayleigh residents. In 1928 the Parish Council

wrote to Essex Police to ask that 'in view of the great difficulty … now entailed … when requiring the aid of the police, a more central site will be established as headquarters'.

SEWERAGE

By 1925 the Parish Council was beginning to accept that a decent sewerage scheme was desirable. In that year there were 'serious complaints' about the lack of a scheme, but finance and arguments continued to delay its implementation.

It took until 1929 for a scheme to get underway and then only thanks to the approval of an unemployment grant, but at least work could now commence.

MORE CHANGE

The Parish Council had achieved a lot since its inception in 1894: a decent water supply; the beginnings of a decent sewerage system; the creation of a Fire Brigade; improved schooling provision; and the introduction of Council houses for the less well-off. However, the town was growing so rapidly that it was felt in many circles that more changes to its administration were required and by 1929 these changes were beginning to loom very large indeed.

Nine

The Years of the Urban District Council

From the 1890s to the 1920s the parishes in the western part of the Rural District regularly sought support from each other in trying to persuade the Rural District or County Councils to accept their point of view. As time wore on they also began to seek increasing autonomy over their own affairs.

During the 1920s, as this pressure grew, it became apparent that some sort of local government reorganisation was inevitable and Rayleigh, once an important town anyway and now growing rapidly in size, began to put its case.

REORGANISATION

From 1924 onwards there was much discussion between the parishes as to how best they might organise themselves to their own advantage. Although most wished to band together in some way, Rayleigh consistently sought independence from everyone. In 1927 the Parish Council convened a parish meeting about the desirability of constituting Rayleigh as an Urban Authority (giving it more powers) and residents voted overwhelmingly in favour.

The County Council meanwhile wanted to group Rayleigh with Hadleigh, Thundersley and Rawreth. The Parish Council replied that 'this Council is of the opinion, and it is desirable, that Rayleigh should itself be constituted an Urban Authority'. Nevertheless, they did allow some room for manoeuvre, stating that they would 'agree to a compromise that Rawreth be included with Rayleigh, subject to the approval of the parish meeting'.

Later that year Rayleigh and Rawreth Parish Councils held a joint meeting and agreed that they would accept a merger if they were not allowed complete independence. Each parish would retain its identity as an electoral ward within the new authority to allow different expenses to continue to be levied for each area.

In October 1928 a Local Inquiry took place and the outcome was the authorised merger of Rayleigh and Rawreth into a new Rayleigh Urban District with effect from 1 October 1929. The Arterial Road was made the official boundary between Rayleigh and Thundersley parishes. Boundary adjustments were also agreed with Hockley and Eastwood, the latter 'moving' New England and Rawreth Hall Woods into Rayleigh. The final meeting of the Parish Council, its minutes taken by the clerk C.E. Judd, who had served in that capacity since the beginning, took place on 23 September 1929.

Crucially, the new Rayleigh Urban District Council had increased administrative powers and for the first time in a long time Rayleigh was no longer subservient to the Rochford Rural District Council.

RAWRETH

Rawreth was a predominantly agricultural parish to the north-west of Rayleigh, straddling the Chelmsford Road (now the old A130) and bordered by Rayleigh and Hockley to the east, the River Crouch at Battlesbridge to the north and Wickford and North Benfleet to the west. The hamlet of Battlesbridge was part of Rawreth parish.

In some ways it was an unusual choice for a partnership, since although the two places were connected by Rawreth Lane, agriculture was

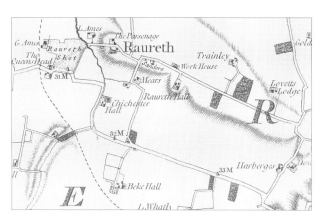

126   Chapman & André's map of Rawreth in 1777, showing the church and some of the farms.

probably the only thing they had in common. Nevertheless, one can see the attraction of a merger for Rawreth residents as Rayleigh was a growing and progressive town, which could bring many benefits.

Rawreth parish was centred on the church of St Nicholas, which had been largely rebuilt in 1882 to the design of the well-known Essex rector-architect, the Rev. Ernest Geldart. Several other historic buildings also survived, including: Tryndehayes, Rawreth Hall and Carter & Saunders Farm in Rawreth Lane; Beke Hall, off the London Road; Beeches and Telfords at Battlesbridge; and a whole range of scattered farmsteads, including Burrells, Dollyman's, Shot, Shotgate and Witherden's (more recently known as Bluehouse) Farms. All of these buildings still survive, along with probably the best-known Rawreth building, Chichester Hall, now the *Chichester Hotel* and Restaurant. The *Carpenters Arms*, a well-known public house, is also in Rawreth.

The name Rawreth means 'heron stream'. The population of the parish in 1931 was 663.

RAYLEIGH URBAN DISTRICT COUNCIL

The new authority had greatly increased powers. It had direct control over sanitation (water supply, drainage and sewerage), highways, burial grounds, allotments, libraries, refuse collection, nuisance control and many other things. Some of these still required the sanction of the County Council, but the new Urban District Council (UDC) clearly had much more control over its own affairs.

The new arrangements had several immediate effects. In Rayleigh the sewerage scheme was postponed for another 12 months, whilst in Rawreth, still largely agricultural, there was the opportunity to start introducing a modern infrastructure – gas, lighting, Council houses, etc. – and to bring the village's services into line with Rayleigh's.

The first chairman of the new authority was the ex-Rayleigh Parish Council chairman, Councillor E.P. Rand, a very active and public-spirited individual. In February 1931, after 18 months at the helm and on being thanked by his fellow councillors for his service, Councillor Rand told them that 'his one hope and desire was to see Rayleigh succeed'. With a local authority career spanning several decades, he did a lot personally to transform this desire into reality.

Councillor Rand was followed as chairman, in a clearly calculated diplomatic move, by the ex-Rawreth Parish Council chairman, Councillor Thomas Todd.

There were 18 councillors on the authority, 12 representing Rayleigh and six Rawreth.

EMERGENCY SERVICES

One of the first acts of the new Council was to replace the fire engine that had been bought in the final years of the Parish Council with a new one. Several companies were invited to demonstrate their machines and in October 1930 the Council entered into a contract with Simonis Ltd for the purchase of a Thorneycroft-Simonis engine. This was duly delivered on 3 October 1931.

In the same month the Council considered the desirability of erecting a purpose-built fire station, opting initially for the erection of a temporary building on the site of some old brickfields in Castle Road. This was constructed by March 1932. The Fire Brigade was still voluntary at this time.

In September 1930 the Council heard from Rayleigh Toc H that they had raised £246 and wanted the Council to use it towards the purchase of 'a new motor ambulance'. The Council supported this proposal and in July 1931 took steps to procure a Ford ambulance at a cost of £350. In 1933 this was stored at the Crown garage. It was replaced by a new Austin ambulance in the late 1930s.

The remote location of the 'police headquarters on the Arterial' was still proving unpopular and by 1938 the police were beginning to get the message. In March 1939 they informed the Council that a new police station was planned for erection in the town centre during the financial year 1942-3, though international events were ultimately to prevent this.

SEWERAGE

By June 1930 the sewerage construction scheme was at last well under way. Its introduction had been helped by an unemployment grant and in that month there were 53 men employed on sewerage construction, 13 of them 'from depressed areas'. The numbers rose even higher over the next few years.

The work was not without its problems, however. Five or six roads were dug up simultaneously, and there were frequent complaints from residents and road users about poor workmanship and disruption to traffic movements. One of the workers even testified against his employers, whom he claimed had mistreated him and encouraged speedy construction at the cost of quality.

Western and eastern disposal works were constructed well out of the town centre, the former off Watery Lane in Rawreth and the latter in the vicinity of New England Wood in Rayleigh. The scheme was formally opened on 19 November 1932.

The sewers only drained Rayleigh, as Rawreth sewerage went into Wickford under an earlier arrangement with Billericay Urban District Council.

HOUSING

Another early decision of the new Council was the demolition in 1930 of Sweep's Row, a terrace of houses off Crown Hill which appears in many early photographs of the town and which was becoming dilapidated.

As time went on, more Council houses were also provided, including some at Weir Gardens and in Pearson's Avenue.

In November 1934 the Council looked for the first time at the question of providing bungalows for 'aged persons'.

ELECTRICITY

Another boon for local residents introduced at this time was electricity.

The old Parish Council had supported the idea for the use of electricity in Rayleigh for lighting and domestic use as early as 1902. Nothing had been done about it, however, and it had taken until 1923, by which time electricity was becoming more widespread, for them to contact the local electricity undertaking, Wickford & District Electricity Supply Company Limited. Representatives from the company had attended a Council meeting in 1924 and, although councillors were impressed with their presentation, they decided to defer a decision on the grounds that the gas company had powers in Rayleigh and that the Wickford supply source was too far away.

Discussions continued throughout the 1920s and correspondence was exchanged with another potential supplier, International Combustion Limited, and various other local authorities to obtain information about their use of electricity.

The final years of the Parish Council saw increased activity on the subject and in July 1929 the County of London Electricity Supply Company attended a meeting to explain what they could do and suggested that they could commence installation of a supply as early as January 1930.

By May 1930, by which time the Parish Council had been replaced by the UDC, electricity installation was well underway, with a major electricity link installed to Rayleigh from Barking. Electricity mains continued to be laid across the District throughout the 1930s.

PUBLIC SERVICES

Several other public services appeared in the 1930s.

There had already been privately-run libraries in the town, but there was still no public library. This was rectified by 1937 when an Essex County Library was in operation at Barringtons, albeit staffed by volunteers.

The County Council had been planning a joint library and health centre in Eastwood Road (opposite Queens Road), but in the event only the latter was built there. Its erection was underway by the summer of 1938.

A 'new Post Office and telephone exchange' was built in the High Road in the early 1930s and telephone boxes were provided throughout the town. Meanwhile, the letterbox at the *Crown* was replaced because it was 'too small to meet the requirements of the District'.

The public toilets at the top of Crown Hill were also opened in the early 1930s.

TRAFFIC

Traffic continued to be a major problem in the town.

In June 1930 it was reported that there was an 'enormous amount of traffic' at the Eastwood Road corner, whilst the following month the Council discussed the desirability of introducing a one-way system in the narrow Bellingham Lane. Authorisation from the Ministry of Transport for the implementation of a system in Bellingham Lane and Church Street was received in May 1937.

Congestion was also growing in the High Street, but in June 1931 the Council decided that 'it would be preferable not to make formal parking places for cars at the moment'. The matter was picked up again in September 1936, when the Council considered for the first time the possibility of providing a car park in the town. However, they concluded in December 1937 that 'at the present time there is no necessity for a car park in this town'.

Some road improvements were, however, permitted by the demolition in the early 1930s of Patmore's bakery, which stood in front of Holy Trinity Church. The site was acquired for road widening, though part was subsequently laid out as a small public garden.

In March 1935 the Council considered providing pedestrian crossings in the High Street, Eastwood Road and at the junction of High Street/Love Lane, all catered for with crossings today.

Outside the town centre improvements were made to Down Hall Road, while further afield a proposal was made by Essex County Council in 1930 to build a new 'Rayleigh Bypass and Spur Road' to the west of the town over land in Rawreth formerly used as allotments. The matter was to drag on for another 35 years.

In March 1936 the Council heard that the County Council was proposing a roundabout to replace the crossroads at Rayleigh Weir, barely a decade old but already a busy junction. This duly took place and in September 1937 neighbouring Benfleet Urban District Council (made up of the old parishes of Benfleet, Hadleigh and Thundersley) wrote seeking support for their proposal to press the County Council to erect traffic lights at the Weir because 'during times of heavy traffic it is almost impossible for pedestrians to cross the Arterial Road at the roundabout'. The Council supported this proposal, but the County Council decided to take no action.

In 1939 further improvements were made with the dualling of the Arterial.

PUBLIC TRANSPORT

By 1932 traffic on the Essex railway mainline had increased so much that the line between London and Shenfield was quadrupled. Six years later automatic signalling was introduced and signal boxes along the Shenfield-Southend line began to close.

Competition between bus companies continued to grow. In 1930 Eastern National was created, though it was traceable in origin back to 1902.

An important local operator in Rayleigh in the 1930s was A.J. Springett, whose licence application in 1931 was strongly supported by the Council on the grounds that 'Mr Springett had done more to accommodate the requirements of the public than any other proprietor' in the town. Benfleet & District Motor Services and New Empress Saloons Ltd were also active.

All this bus activity contributed to the growing congestion in the High Street, with buses from Southend turning outside the *Crown* and those from Hockley parking or turning opposite the *Chequers*. Rayleigh station was a key terminus for many bus routes and was destined to become an important link in the local transport network.

THE CINEMA

By this stage there was a cinema in the town, just off the High Street in Bellingham Lane. It was called the *Cosy Talkie Theatre*. In February 1931 councillors regretted that they had to refuse 'proposed alterations to Rayleigh cinema' due to the narrowness of the road there.

The *Cosy* was replaced in 1937 by a new cinema on the same site, the *Regal*. This was owned by the prestigious Astoria chain and could seat 696 people.

The *Regal* became renowned for its high standard of personal service and served Rayleigh people faithfully for 36 years until its closure on 29 September 1973. The last films shown were *Dirty Harry* and *Klute*.

In 1937 the cinema car park, the only sizeable one in the town, was jealously eyed by the Council for possible use as a public car park. Nothing happened about this at the time, but the idea of providing public car parking in Bellingham Lane was established and would later come to fruition.

RECREATION AND LEISURE

In 1924 the old Parish Council had considered the provision of a recreation ground for the town. The ongoing development meant that land was being swallowed up, and there was clearly a need to protect some of it from development. Councillors drew up a shortlist of possible sites and after several site visits finally selected land at Fairview, off Hockley Road. Arrangements were not concluded until the UDC had taken over, but the ground

THE COSY TALKIE THEATRE
RAYLEIGH
CONTINUOUS FROM 2.15

SPECIAL JUBILEE WEEK PROGRAMME

MONDAY, TUESDAY & WEDNESDAY
George Arliss in
THE LAST GENTLEMAN
and STANLEY LUPINO in
YOU MADE ME LOVE YOU

THURSDAY, FRIDAY & SATURDAY
Gracie Fields in
SING AS WE GO
and TOM TYLER in
BEYOND THE BORDER

127 An advertisement for the *Cosy Talkie Theatre*, predecessor of the *Regal Cinema*, 1935.

was to prove a valuable amenity, with facilities for tennis, cricket and bowls and a children's playground. It was also regularly used for sporting events and entertainment.

One of the earliest events celebrated there was King George V's Silver Jubilee in 1935. This featured the usual activities of organised games, sports, a religious service, a tea for children, flags and fireworks.

In June 1937 Rayleigh Ratepayers Association marked the next major royal occasion, that of King George VI's coronation, with the presentation of a chain of office to the Council chairman.

The UDC recognised early on that more playing fields were needed and in 1936 it identified open spaces in London Road, Watch Field, Mill Field and Hambro Hill as possible sites. Councillors wisely planned to provide open spaces for a population of 20,000, although the actual figure at the time was only around six thousand.

Other popular leisure amenities of the period included the Co-operative Hall in the High Street and the Clissold Hall in Eastwood Road. Both hosted music and dancing. There was also an annual carnival.

One attraction which some residents did not welcome was a greyhound track, which opened in the vicinity of London Road/Down Hall

ESSEX

About three-quarters of a mile from Rayleigh Station. 7 miles from Southend.

PARTICULARS AND CONDITIONS OF SALE OF THE
COMFORTABLE AND MEDIUM-SIZED
FREEHOLD FAMILY RESIDENCE
known as

Fairview
RAYLEIGH

Pleasant and Healthy Position, about 220 feet up, Fine Open Views.
Approached by Carriage Sweep and containing : Entrance Hall, Four Reception
Rooms, Principal and Secondary Staircases, Seven Bed Rooms, Bath Room
and Compact Domestic Offices.
Company's Gas and Water.   *Telephone.*
GARAGES.   CHAUFFEUR'S QUARTERS.   STABLING.

Very Attractive Pleasure Grounds

Lawns and Hard Tennis Court, Kitchen Garden, etc., in all about

FIVE ACRES
Also
Lot 2. A Pair of Well-Built Cottages
and
Lot 3. Over 15½ Acres of Valuable Building Land
WITH VACANT POSSESSION.

HAMPTON & SONS

Will offer the above for Sale by Auction
At The St. James' Estate Rooms, 20, St. James' Square, London, S.W.1
On TUESDAY, 19th JUNE, 1928
At 2.30 p.m. (unless previously disposed of). In THREE LOTS.

Solicitors : Messrs. MARTIN & NICHOLSON, 29, Queen Street, London, E.C.4.
Particulars and Conditions of Sale may be obtained from the Auctioneers,
HAMPTON & SONS,   **20, St. James' Square, London, S.W.1.**

Branches : Wimbledon. 'Phone 0080.   Telephone :
Hampstead. 'Phone 2727.   Regent 7500.

128 A sale advertisement for Fairview in 1928. The land was purchased by Rayleigh Parish Council for the town's first recreation ground.

1910 - 1935

To Commemorate the Silver Jubilee
of the Accession of Their Majesties
The King and Queen

May 6th, 1935.

LONG MAY THEY REIGN

Issued by the Rayleigh Silver Jubilee Celebrations Committee

129 The programme of activities for the celebration in Rayleigh of the Silver Jubilee of King George V in 1935.

Road in late 1932 or early 1933. Residents in Down Hall Road regularly complained to the Council about barking dogs. The track had closed down by February 1934.

In 1936 the Council considered a proposal for a golf course on land to the north of Fishers Farm. They were uncertain as to the desirability of this but they did take steps to retain the land as open space, zoning it for non-development.

In 1938 the subject was raised again when the owners of Turret House approached the Council to offer the building as a clubhouse and the surrounding land as a golf course. This time councillors generally favoured the idea, but the looming war led to any decision on it being postponed in March 1939.

RELIGION

Reverend Fryer was succeeded at Holy Trinity by Reverend A.C. Sowter, who was formally inducted on 4 January 1932.

In 1931 the Rayleigh Congregational Church celebrated its 21st anniversary and raised money to carry out improvements. The Rev. Macdonald, who produced a commemorative booklet to mark the occasion, left for Birmingham in 1934 and was replaced in 1935 by the Rev. Alan Wood, who came to Rayleigh direct from college.

Changes were also afoot at the Methodist Church. In March 1930 church representatives met to discuss the inadequacy of the existing premises. Increasing attendance meant that a larger building was desirable and they began to look for an alternative site.

130 The opening of the new Methodist Church in Eastwood Road in 1934.

After exploring several possibilities, they opted for a site owned by a Methodist syndicate in Eastwood Road. The new church was opened in 1934 and the old church in the High Road was sold to the Salvation Army.

The 1930s also saw the re-establishment of another strand of religious worship in the town with the foundation of Our Lady of Ransom Catholic Church in London Hill, under Father James Hemming.

Financial problems meant that construction had to be halted shortly after the laying of the foundation stone, but the incomplete building was nevertheless officially 'opened' by Bishop Arthur Doubleday on the feast day of Our Lady of Ransom, 24 September 1934. Rayleigh was the headquarters of local Catholic worship and

ministers from the town were often sent to provide services in surrounding towns and villages.

A NEW SCHOOL

By 1930 school accommodation was again becoming cramped and it was recognised that a new senior school was required. The Council considered several possible sites, including Weir Gardens, which was then under development.

In April 1934, however, the Essex Education Committee wrote to say that they were planning the construction of a 480-pupil senior school in Hockley Road. This was duly built, being officially opened in November 1937 by J. W. Burrows, chairman of the Southend Higher Education Committee.

131   Rayleigh High Street, c.1930s, showing on the left the old Council Offices.

This school, which in 1967 would become Fitzwimarc, was designed to be easily adaptable to accommodate more children in the future if required.

COUNCIL OFFICES

The first UDC meetings had taken place at the Council Schools in Love Lane, there being as yet no purpose-built Council chamber in the town. As soon as the new secondary school opened, however, Council meetings were transferred there.

In the early 1930s the Council offices were housed in a variety of buildings, principally at the top end of the High Street. Councillors recognised early on that they needed purpose-built offices and spent much time looking for a suitable site. Twice they thought about purchasing the redundant *Golden Lion* hotel and converting it, but decided against it. Other

sites inspected included London Hill, Eastwood Road (next to the Peculiar People's Chapel), Rayleigh House and Barringtons. In July 1934 they made a concerted effort to examine every possible option and had 18 sites on their list.

A decision was delayed, however, until further local authority reorganisation had been completed.

LOCAL AUTHORITY
REORGANISATION

Despite the fact that the UDC had been created only in 1929, the 1930s were filled with proposals from the County Council and others for further local administrative reorganisation.

Amongst them was a proposal in 1932 from Southend Borough Council, which was in the process of adding Eastwood parish to its administrative area, for the transfer of the area around Eastwood Rise and Eastwood Lodge into the UDC. The latter's councillors accepted this proposal and the transfer took place on 1 April 1934.

Within the Urban District it was also time for a review of operations to even up the administrative inequities between Rayleigh and Rawreth. The District was still divided into two wards of unequal size and representation, covering the old parish areas. Rayleigh still had 12 councillors and Rawreth six.

In January 1936 the UDC clerk, Henry Broadhurst, submitted a report on possible options regarding the redistribution of the parish into wards. He proposed the dissolution of the old Rawreth civic parish and the enlargement of the old Rayleigh civic parish to form one large civic parish whose boundaries would be coterminous with those of the Urban District. The whole District could then be reorganised into six similar-sized wards, each with three councillors.

Mr Broadhurst's view was that 18 councillors was actually too many for the size of the District, but he was reluctant to advocate a reduction as he felt that any attempt later to increase it would have to be fought for. He proposed the redistribution of wards by geographical area rather than population, but acknowledged that this meant that at the current stage of development only three of those wards had buildings in them that could be used as polling stations; the other three had only farms and houses and most of the area was in any case still largely agricultural. However, 'both Rayleigh and Rawreth,' he wrote, 'are possessed of great possibilities so far as development is concerned and … I believe that the time is not far distant when rapid development will commence over the whole of this area'.

He wasn't wrong, and the seeds were sown for later ward reorganisation.

INDUSTRY AND SERVICES

In July 1933 the Council reached agreement with neighbouring Benfleet Urban District Council to designate the Weir area on both sides of the Arterial for light industry. There was some disagreement as to how far this area should extend and in July 1936 Rayleigh UDC approved a factory manufacturing soft goods and employing 200 people near Little Wheatley Farm. However, the government overruled this and recommended a complete review of potential industrial sites in the Urban District, especially sites close to Rayleigh station. The Council was already of the view by this stage that any factories in the District should be 'for light industry only and not for noxious trades'.

Meanwhile, the Council had begun operating a refuse tip in a former brickfield in Castle Road. By 1938 this was filling up and councillors began to look for alternative sites.

By the early 1930s gas supply for Rayleigh had been taken over by the Gas, Light & Coke Company. An additional site had been acquired at the bottom of Crown Hill near the railway station and a gasholder was erected there.

BUSINESS

Businesses in 1930s Rayleigh continued to prosper, not least in the construction industry. Builders J.T. Byford, Treganza & Moore, A.H. Poole and C.S. Wiggins & Sons all benefited from the continued growth of the town and between them built much of 20th-century Rayleigh.

Other businesses active during this period included Harding's sausage & ice cream factory in Bull Lane and the Bellingham House Cafe, Grant Brothers furniture removers, Hinksman's garage, Howard's Dairies, H. Mann's grocers, Parr's butchers and Sansom's gentlemen's outfitters in the town centre. Of the national chains, Barclays and Westminster Banks had premises in the High Street and International Tea Stores and the London Co-operative Society were also present. There was even a *Rayleigh & Wickford Gazette*.

A sign of the times was the presence of Rayleigh Radio & Gramophone Stores, radio being a relatively recent innovation.

WEBSTER'S MEADOW

In March 1936 the Council was informed that Norman Webster was selling an area of land known as 'Webster's Meadow' which lay behind the shops on the eastern side of the High Street between Eastwood Road and Bull Lane. Mr Webster wanted to know if the Council was interested in buying the land, which due to its central location represented a prime site in the expanding town.

The Council was very interested and councillors had many ideas for the use of the land. This included using the Eastwood Road frontage as a site for Council Offices, the location for which had still not been resolved. At a meeting of the General Purposes Committee in May 1936 councillors reported that 'some members may be of the opinion that Municipal Buildings should be erected in the High Street, but we would point out that it is now impossible to acquire vacant land in the High Street, and even if it was available the price thereof would be prohibitive'.

After protracted negotiations, during which the price and the size of the area to be purchased could not be agreed upon, the Council decided in November 1936 to seek a Compulsory Purchase Order for the Eastwood Road frontage. This was to be the first of two such Orders, the second relating to using the bulk of the land for recreational purposes. Both were confirmed by the government in 1938.

Mr Webster wanted a road to be included in the scheme to give him access to his property and the Council, already contemplating a road there itself, agreed in principle to this.

GROWTH

Every year from the early 1930s onwards the local Medical Officer for Health, Dr Norman Lorraine, reported on various social and healthcare aspects of the District, including population figures. His mid-year population estimate for 1932 was 6,678. By 1936 this had risen to 7,265.

The Reverend Fryer, writing in 1932, noted that there had been much development by this stage since his first book in 1908. Many of the original, ancient roads in the town 'are being altered and straightened, and trees and hedges which obscure the view cut down, all

a necessary matter, maybe, but one which is assuredly being done at the loss of much of the charm and beauty of Nature.

'New roads are being constantly made in the district, and new houses and bungalows built along them.'

Estate agents were promoting the health and amenities of the Urban District and 'there is every probability of Rayleigh doubling its population within the next few years'.

An increasing number of residents was commuting to London and 'agriculture has departed from the neighbourhood'. Rayleigh was becoming a dormitory and retirement town.

'It may,' predicted the Reverend Fryer, in his customarily accurate way, 'be safely said that a town so easily reached from London is destined to go on growing … The land around the town will … be swallowed up by the house estate promoters … [and] Rayleigh will approximate more and more to the condition of a suburb of London as houses multiply in number.'

The 4th Edition of the Ordnance Survey map (1938) provides a good pictorial view of the results of some of this growth.

THE SECOND WORLD WAR

In June 1935 the Council minutes recorded the first signs of another impending war, when the Council gave its support to a motion from Purfleet Urban District Council, pressing the government 'to pursue a policy of peace' regarding 'the present grave international complications'. From then on preparations for war began to dominate proceedings, especially the matter of air raid precautions (ARP), and by January 1939 there were 170 ARP volunteers in the Urban District.

The Council received visits and advice from top military strategists, plus government circulars about such things as the use of maroons to sound a warning, lights out, accommodation, hospitals, medical equipment, personnel, fire and ambulance provision, anti-gas measures and food and fuel control. In January 1938 a joint conference was held with Benfleet and Billericay Urban District Councils to consider a site for an aerodrome. None was ever built.

132 The Fourth Edition Ordnance Survey Map of 1938, showing north-eastern Rayleigh. This map makes for interesting comparison with the 3rd Edition of 1923 (see p.103). A few more streets have appeared – Queens Road, Kings Road, Highfield Crescent – but the area is still largely rural.

Local allotments, the Senior School playing fields and the gardens of the town's Council houses were all commandeered for food production.

On 8-9 July and 9-10 August 1939 the Council took part in a night-time blackout exercise for the RAF, while in November it had the grisly task of identifying additional mortuary accommodation for the expected

disasters ahead. Two of the town's leading funeral directors – A.R. Adams and H. Witham & Sons (both still in operation today) – offered their premises for the purpose. Later in the war the Council set aside land at the cemetery for the burial of enemy airmen.

An air-raid siren was installed at the fire station in Castle Road, but in September 1940 this had to be augmented by whistles in the

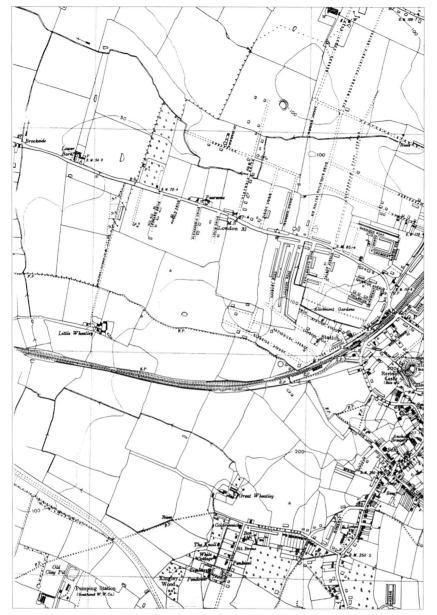

133 Western Rayleigh from the Fourth Edition Ordnance Survey Map of 1938, showing the A127, the railway line and embryonic development off London Road.

relatively new Grange Estate area (to the west of the railway line) as residents there could not hear it.

The first major incident came on 22 November 1939 when the siren was sounded due to anti-aircraft fire. By this stage, public air-raid shelters had been provided behind the *Regal* cinema and various similar measures taken around the town. Anderson and Morrison shelters were also provided for residents as the war wore on.

As with the First World War, troops were again billeted in the town and various exercises took place there. One of the earliest was the 156th A.A. Battery of the Royal Artillery, who had left by early spring 1940 and wrote in March thanking the Council and inhabitants for the warm welcome they had received.

134 The headquarters of the local Spitfire Fund in Rayleigh in 1940. Throughout the war there were several fund-raising drives to raise money for urgently needed military equipment.

In May 1940 Councillor Mrs Frances Cottee became the first female chairman of the UDC. Several Council staff and, of course, many Rayleigh inhabitants joined the Local Defence Volunteers, forerunners of the Home Guard. Later, Rayleigh branches of the Air Training Corps and the Women's Voluntary Service were formed.

The Council also supported several major national initiatives. In September 1940, with the Battle of Britain on everyone's minds, councillors agreed a request from local voluntary associations to inaugurate a Spitfire Fund. Rayleigh was on the receiving end during the Battle, but aerial dogfights were evidently still something of a novelty, for it was reported that 'whilst attending a fire caused by a crashed aeroplane on 7th September … the Brigade was greatly hampered by the sight-seeing public'.

The fire brigade was extremely active during the war and a well-known local company of the time, H. Dowling & Sons, provided a lorry and driver for the use of the brigade. In November 1939 water from the moat around Rayleigh Mount was earmarked for use in fire-fighting. Water tanks were later provided at strategic locations around the town.

Air raids continued throughout the war and on 20 October 1940 five members of the Moss family, related to a former councillor but not then resident in the town, were killed in one. They are buried at Rayleigh cemetery. In November damage was sustained by Lime House, one of the older buildings in the parish.

In 1941 a community feeding centre known as the British Restaurant was established in Eastwood Road. Other local communal kitchen facilities were also pressed into use, while propaganda and public information films were shown at the *Regal*.

In December 1941 the Council was asked to identify surplus railings in the town which could be melted down and used to manufacture weapons. They commissioned

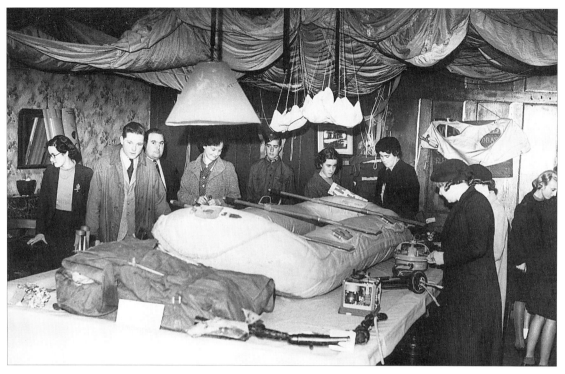

135 An exhibition of equipment from a German plane, on display in Rayleigh for fund-raising purposes in 1940.

a survey, identifying several properties, some of whose owners were not impressed! With recycling a priority, they also oversaw regular collections of wastepaper, bottles, rags, metal, food and bones.

In April 1942 Rayleigh residents again rose to the fundraising challenge and collected enough money to sponsor a ship for Warship Week. Representatives from the chosen ship – Motor Torpedo Boat 207 – came to the town the following year to thank local people for their achievement. The ship was decommissioned in 1947.

The Council recognised the importance of entertainment for keeping up the spirits and in the summer of 1942 laid on several dances at the playing fields and concerts at the senior school. The Crown Hall was also used. The following year there were plans for a garden and poultry show in aid of the Red Cross and a concert by an American band was held at the senior school. Many events were encouraged

by the energetic entertainments committee chairman, Councillor Rees, who unfortunately passed away before the war had ended.

In the early hours of Thursday 15 April 1943 there was a major air raid on the District, with Daws Heath Road very badly hit. Several houses were demolished and their inhabitants buried beneath the debris. Dr Bateman attended many of the injured and was later awarded the MBE for his work.

At a Council meeting four days later 'Councillor Huxtable … briefly referred to the somewhat severe damage which the District recently suffered from an enemy air attack, and members of the Council stood in silence for a few moments as a tribute to the inhabitants of the District who had unfortunately lost their lives'. The owners of the *Regal* cinema, and its manager, Mr J.E. Lake, were amongst the many who gave to the subsequent distress fund.

October 1944 saw several major attacks on the District as the Germans launched their

136 Damage caused by an air raid in 1944.

137 More damage caused by an air raid in 1944, this time to Rayleigh House.

138 The remains of the bathchair from the 'Bathchair Bombing' in 1943.

'revenge weapons' – the V1 and V2 rockets – as their last throw of the dice in a war they were losing. There were major incidents on 11, 12 and 21 October, the latter claiming the lives of serving Councillor and former UDC chairman, William Hollinghurst, his wife Margaret and several other Rayleigh residents. In the early hours of 15 November 1944 there was another attack, with three people being killed and several others injured. Further large-

scale attacks followed in January and March 1945.

Nevertheless, by May 1945 the Germans had surrendered and the war was won. Councillors had already recalled 'with pride the ready response made by so many of our people to the national call and their unselfish devotion to duty'.

Victory in Europe (VE) Day was celebrated on 8 May 1945 and there was rejoicing in the streets. A Victory Fund & Welcome Home Fund was established to mark the occasion and to help financially those returning from the war.

The Council recognised the sacrifices made by many Rayleigh people during the country's hour of need and put on record its admiration for 'the outstanding manner in which the serious results occasioned by the enemy incidents … were overcome both with expedition and efficiency [and] brought early relief to the unfortunate casualties and created that feeling of confidence which was an integral feature in the welfare and daily life of the community'.

Councillor E.P. and Mrs Rand financed the purchase and planting of an avenue of trees in the cemetery in memory of Rayleigh people killed in the war, the names of whom are listed on the roll of honour at the Royal British Legion in Church Street. A memorial garden was laid out on the site of Patmore's and a lychgate later erected at Holy Trinity to help perpetuate the memory of those involved.

THE 'BATHCHAIR BOMBING'

The use of high explosives during the Second World War in Rayleigh was unfortunately not confined to attacks by the Germans. A most bizarre incident took place on 23 July 1943 when Archibald Brown, a member of the T.J. Brown & Sons milling family who owned and operated Rayleigh windmill, was murdered with an anti-tank grenade mine.

Mr Brown, a cantankerous invalid confined to a wheelchair after a motorcycle accident, was being pushed along the Hockley Road near Gattens by his attendant, Nurse Mitchell, when his wheelchair exploded, killing him and injuring his nurse.

The subsequent police investigation discovered that Mr Brown's son, Private Eric Brown, who was on compassionate leave home from military service, had placed an anti-tank grenade mine under the seat of the wheelchair with the intention of killing his father because he was so overbearing. Eric was found 'guilty but insane' on 4 November 1943 and jailed for life.

POST-WAR HOUSE-BUILDING

In April 1943 the government wrote to the Council to ask them to think about their post-war house-building programme. Over 1,200 houses had been damaged in the District during the war. One of the most prominent, Rayleigh

139 Hockley Road in 1943. This photograph was taken by the police during investigation into the Bathchair Bombing. Damage to the road surface caused by the explosion can be seen on the left-hand side of the road about halfway between the viewer and the car.

140   Rayleigh High Street, *c.*1945. Note the increase of traffic in the town centre.

House, which had been part-converted into six flats in the 1930s, was so dilapidated in November 1945 that it was estimated that it would take six months to repair.

The Council's favoured sites for new housing were Weir Gardens in Rayleigh and Bedloes Corner in Rawreth. Another major location identified for new homes was the Bull Lane/Louise Road/Jubilee Road/Trinity Road/Kings Road/Queens Road/Meadowside area, where improvements were required in any case to the road network between Bull Lane and Eastwood Road.

Later, councillors looked at sites in Hambro Hill, Church Road, Warwick Road, The Chase, London Road and Down Hall Road in Rayleigh and Goose Cottages in Battlesbridge. Many more local authority and private developments would follow, including Picton Close and Gardens, built on the site of Picton House.

In the year 1949-50, 50 houses were built in the Urban District; 250 more were planned for the period 1951-6 and a further 1,500 for the period 1956-71. Anderson Brothers, Blower Brothers and Mr E. Trippier were all active local builders in the early 1950s.

Another housing initiative came from Mr T. W. Finch and his sister Mrs E.J. Seed, who left land and money for the construction of 12 bungalows for aged people in Eastwood Road in what is now Finchfield.

The post-war period saw continued growth in the town's population. This rose steadily throughout the 1940s, reaching 9,388 in 1951.

In the year ending 31 March 1955 Rayleigh was listed as having the most number of private houses under construction per 1000 population of any UDC in England and Wales. Councillors noted the report 'with satisfaction'.

141 Bull Lane, *c.*1945. Despite increasing development, parts of the town were still fairly rural.

The population was now into five figures, with an estimate of over 19,000 for 1971.

INDUSTRY

After the war the Council began to think more about local industry.

Although gas was still the principal power source, electricity was coming more into use. An electricity transformer station already existed near the station and by 1947 the Council was considering replacing the gas street-lighting with electricity, though some parts of Rawreth were still not served by either. Electric sodium street lighting was finally provided in the town centre in the late 1950s.

Despite this, a second gasholder was erected near the station in 1950 by the North Thames Gas Board, by now successors to the Gas, Light & Coke Company, as part of a scheme to improve gas supply throughout south-east Essex. The Eastern Electricity Board was introduced around the same time.

The Castle Road refuse tip was giving cause for concern. It was full by 1950 and the Council began to use a new site in Hambro Hill.

Sites for industry were also being considered, with the Council still favouring land to the west of the Weir. However, in 1947 the government refused permission for an industrial estate west of the Weir cutting and asked the UDC to review the whole area regarding their industrial requirements. They did so, and by 1952 there were 43 factories in the District, including some in Rawreth Lane. Businesses included Bakelite & plastic manufacture, furniture manufacture, horticulture and 'a large mousery where innumerable species of mice are bred for scientific research purposes'. In that year 98.2 per cent of the District was supplied with water and 87 per cent was connected to the sewerage system.

Businesses in the town centre in the 1950s included Woolworths, Frost's and the Saddlers Restaurant, while a new automatic telephone exchange was planned to replace the manual one by 1960.

THE EMERGENCY SERVICES

There were changes, too, for the emergency services.

The war had seen the introduction of an Auxiliary Fire Service alongside Rayleigh Fire Brigade and then, in 1941, the creation of a new National Fire Service. In 1944 Fire Brigade property was transferred to the National Fire Service and two years later the Service was transferred from government to Essex County Council control.

In 1947 the Fire Service Act caused a county force to be formed officially and thus ended

142 Rayleigh High Street, *c*.1950s. Note the modern lighting columns, which look somewhat out of place alongside the older houses and vehicles.

local responsibility for fire-fighting provision. The complement of firemen for Rayleigh was 12 – all to be 'retained', i.e. part-time, a system which continues to this day. In 1973 a new fire station was opened in Castle Road, continuing the tradition of Fire Service presence there.

The location of the police at the Weir had already been causing residents some irritation and there was relief in September 1940 when it was announced that they would shortly be moving back to the High Street. This move did indeed take place, but in the late 1940s the new police station was frequently left unmanned and this led to further complaints. The police responded in part by introducing a radio car for night patrols in late 1949.

The town was to see several successive police stations after this, the present one a large modern building erected as a regional station.

In May 1945 the town still had its own ambulance. However, in spring 1950 ambulance services were centralised at Thundersley and there was no longer a need for local provision.

RELIGION

In 1945 the Rev. Sowter was succeeded at Holy Trinity by the Rev. C.F. Carver, who made his presence felt immediately by asking the UDC

for permission to build a new church hall adjacent to the Rectory. Permission was granted. The Church of St Michael was also founded during the Rev. Carver's incumbency.

The Rev. Carver was succeeded in 1956 by the Rev. George W. Hatch, who also served as a canon of Chelmsford Cathedral. The Rev. Hatch oversaw the sale of the Parish Rooms to finance the construction of the new church hall and went on to serve at Rayleigh until 1982.

At the Baptist Church there was some clearing up to be done as the chapel was damaged by the October 1944 air raids. Services were held temporarily in the old British School next door as the roof of the chapel was unsafe.

Increasing development on the Grange Estate west of the railway line prompted the Baptists to establish a Grange Mission Project in 1946 to spread the word of Baptism to that part of the town and thoughts turned to the construction of a new church there.

However, in 1954 Wiggins built a chapel in the vicinity which became the Grange Free Church. This made plans for another church somewhat redundant and the Baptists decided to donate land they owned nearby to the Essex Baptists Association.

The Congregational Church was also affected by the war. Troops occupied the Caley Hall and the kitchen and many worshippers served in the forces. Former minister, the Rev. MacDonald, served as a padre in the Middle East. Recovery from the effects of the war only began to be felt during the late 1950s.

In 1959 the Rev. Hubert Smith was inducted and arrived just in time to oversee the celebrations for the church's 50th anniversary the following year. A commemorative booklet was produced which included a message from the Rev. F.W. Bell, Minister-secretary of the Essex Congregational Union, who observed: 'How much the world has changed since 1910 and how much Rayleigh has changed, too!'.

Another greeting came from Councillor Ernie Lane, chairman of the UDC and himself a member of the Church. Councillor Lane would go on to write two books about Rayleigh (one in conjunction with UDC clerk, Mr C.E. Fitzgerald) and become well-known in the town for his interest in its history.

The Rev. Smith was succeeded by the Rev. Terence Willis, whose tenure coincided with a momentous event in the life of the Congregational Church – its merger with the Presbyterian Church of England to form the United Reformed Church. This was ratified by Act of Parliament in 1972.

At the Catholic Church Father Hemming's tenure lasted until 1951. He was succeeded by Canon Thomas Smith who stayed until 1958 when he was appointed to Brentwood Cathedral. Father Smith was succeeded by Father Andrew Dorricott, who is still the parish priest today.

The church building was still at this stage incomplete and the arrival of Father Dorricott prompted a renewed impetus which finally led to its completion in 1962-5. The first mass in the completed building was celebrated on 8 December 1965 and the church was consecrated by Bishop Bernard Wall on 1 June 1967.

This period also saw the establishment of a foundation of the Cloyne Sisters of Mercy, an Ireland-based group, and the Church and the

Sisters jointly built a Catholic Primary School in Little Wheatley Chase. This, and the Sisters' convent building, were both opened in 1966.

By this stage several other denominations had appeared in the town and more churches of all denominations would follow.

RAYLEIGH STADIUM

A new type of entertainment came to Rayleigh in the late 1940s – motorcycle speedway. A short-lived and apparently unconnected season of races had taken place at Little Wheatley Farm in the summer of 1939 (much to the Council's dissatisfaction), but this had evidently stopped when war broke out.

In 1946, however, the Council heard that neighbouring Benfleet UDC had received a planning application for the construction of a sports stadium on their side of the Arterial Road at Rayleigh Weir. Perhaps recalling their stance in 1939, Rayleigh councillors decided to oppose it and were most unhappy when they heard that Benfleet had approved the application. The decision went to an inquiry, held in Thundersley in the summer of 1947, and the Government decided in favour of the applicants. Still clearly piqued, Rayleigh councillors resolved on the spot that no such stadiums would ever be allowed in their district.

They were still resolute in their opposition in November 1948 when the stadium company announced that it was considering changing its name to 'Rayleigh Weir Stadium Limited'. The Council did not 'favour the name of Rayleigh being associated with the stadium, in view of the fact that the stadium itself is not situated within the urban district of Rayleigh'.

Despite the Council's opposition, construction of the stadium went ahead and in 1948 an ex-bomber pilot called Frank Arnold was given permission to set up a speedway track there.

Although the stadium was outside the Urban District, the Weir area was by then generally regarded as being 'in Rayleigh' and it still is today. The speedway team was consequently given the name 'Rayleigh Rockets', no doubt to the Council's chagrin. Its initial line-up

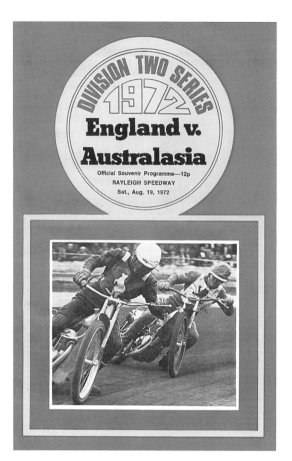

143 A photograph of a speedway programme for the England versus Australasia meeting held at Rayleigh Weir on 19 August 1972.

comprised a mixture of established stars and up-and-coming riders and the team officially entered the national league in 1949. The opening fixture against Leicester was watched by a crowd of twelve thousand.

Over the next 25 years the team competed in various competitions with extremely variable results, sometimes challenging for the title, sometimes seriously underperforming and sometimes coming close to folding. There was also briefly a second team, Rayleigh Rovers.

In August 1948 there were complaints about buses queueing in the High Road as they waited to take people from the stadium. On other occasions the *Weir Hotel*, 'a popular halt for coaches' in its own right, seemed almost swamped with traffic and people.

Greyhound racing also took place at the stadium.

The story ended in 1973 when the stadium site was sold for development. It is now occupied by Sainsbury's supermarket. A reminder of it survives, however, in the road name, Stadium Way.

WEBSTER'S MEADOW

In the town centre, discussions over the acquisition of Webster's Meadow had been put on the back-burner throughout the Second World War. However, in 1950 negotiations were reopened and the Council decided to proceed with the acquisition of the land in accordance with the two 1938 Compulsory Purchase Orders, i.e. for the main meadow itself and for the Eastwood Road frontage. They also decided to press for the remaining strip of land, which backed onto the rear of the High Street properties. The King George's Playing Field Foundation promised a grant towards the cost as part of a programme of providing such fields in memory of King George V.

Webster's Meadow offered many possibilities. It was a large, central site and the growing town had need of several fundamental community services. These included the Council Offices, a community centre, a doctor's surgery and a bus station. All were suggested for Webster's Meadow.

The bus station proposal was the most short-lived. It arose as a possible solution to the 'serious congestion' being caused by buses waiting in the High Street between Crown Hill and Eastwood Road. In 1951 a conference took place between the Council and representatives of the three main bus companies, WMS, Eastern National and City. However, the companies 'were unanimous in their opinion that there was no necessity to provide for a bus station in Rayleigh' and the plan folded.

The question of the location for the Council Offices was also soon resolved (see below) and councillors decided ultimately to retain most of the land as public open space. However, the strip behind the High Street properties was

144 An aerial photograph of King George's Playing Field, formerly Webster's Meadow. This was an important town centre site and discussions about it rumbled on for several decades from the 1930s.

later built on with a new road, Webster's Way, and a car park, opened in 1969.

One of the first events to be celebrated on the new King George's Field (as Webster's Meadow became known) was the coronation of Queen Elizabeth II in 1953.

COUNCIL BUSINESS

Resolution of the dilemma over the best location for the Council Offices came in April 1952 when the Clerk reported that Barringtons was on the market. Councillors were immediately in favour and negotiations began on the acquisition of the site.

On 19 May 1952 the surveyor reported that 'the siting and accommodation available is such that it would be extremely difficult to purchase a building in Rayleigh that would be more suitable for Council offices'.

In January 1953 councillors learned that some boardroom furniture of 'outstanding quality' had become available at St John's Hospital in Halifax, though when fully laid out this would be too large for the existing premises. They therefore agreed to build a new extension to Barringtons 'consisting of a properly laid out Council chamber in which this stately furniture

could be arranged in a most attractive form and of which the Council would be justly proud'.

Councillors were keen to move into their new offices during coronation year and the foundation stone for the new extension was laid in that year by the then Council chairman, W. Victor Curtis. Councillor Curtis was chairman several times and had been active in public affairs in Rayleigh since King George V's Silver Jubilee in 1935.

The accommodation was finally ready in 1954 and the first Council meeting was held there on 22 March.

The deal for the acquisition of Barringtons included continuation of the existing market and the provision of a public car park, something which was becoming acutely necessary in the town.

In December 1962 the Council was granted its own coat-of-arms, with the motto 'We Work for the Future'. These were formally presented in May 1963.

A second extension at Barringtons would later be needed as the workload grew.

In 1949 a Local Inquiry took place to consider increasing the number of electoral wards in the Urban District. This recommended

the division of the District into six wards –
Castle, Grange, Rawreth, Trinity, Wheatley and
Whitehouse. Each of these was to have three
councillors. Five of the wards were in the old
Rayleigh parish and just one was in the old
Rawreth parish, a clear indication of where
most of the growth was taking place.

The wards were officially adopted for the
1950 elections.

Today, with additional population growth
in the centre, there are eight wards across the
town.

EDUCATION

Post-war education facilities in Rayleigh
were destined to mushroom as a result of the
Education Acts of 1944 and 1946.

In 1947 councillors received a report
recommending several major changes to local
education provision, including the enlargement
of the junior and senior schools and the closure
of Rawreth School, which would be replaced by
a new school at the Rawreth end of Rawreth
Lane. Another new secondary school (as senior
schools were now called) was to be built at the
Rayleigh end of London Road. These needs
were ultimately fulfilled to a degree by the Park
and Sweyne Park Schools respectively.

School accommodation was so short in 1956
that the Parish and British Legion Halls were
both used as additional classrooms and over
the next five decades existing schools would be
expanded and new schools built to cater for the
increasing number of children in the town. This
would include Rayleigh's first and only 60s-style
tower block, opened at Fitzwimarc in 1970.

The Essex Education Committee also had
a presence in the town by the mid-1950s,
occupying Brooklands in Hockley Road.

TRAFFIC

Car ownership was also increasing and it
was becoming clear that car parks were now
essential in the town centre. In 1955 the
Council looked at a number of possible sites.
Bellingham Lane, Webster's Way, Barringtons,
Castle Road and improvements at the railway
station were ultimately chosen.

Improvements were also made to several
road junctions, including High Street/Crown
Hill/Eastwood Road, and various traffic-light
options were considered and rejected. In 1970
a one-way system was proposed for the town
centre, with traffic going north through the
High Street and south along Webster's Way.
This was tried for three years from 1972 and
although it was unpopular and emotive for
some the arrangement was made permanent
at the end of 1975.

Outside the town centre there were changes
to the alignment of the Chelmsford Road at
Rawreth and by 1965 the long-proposed new
Spur Road from the *Carpenters Arms* to the
Arterial was finally opened, creating a new
roundabout in London Road in what had
been the old Rawreth parish and providing a
much-needed western bypass for Rayleigh.

PUBLIC TRANSPORT

There were big changes too in the bus world,
with the advent in 1951 of the British Transport
Commission. Eastern National assumed control
of WMS and the once-familiar red livery of the
latter began to disappear from the streets.

Another big operator was Southend
Corporation. From the mid-1950s onwards the
Corporation took over some Rayleigh routes
and their blue and cream buses also became a
familiar sight in the town. Other smaller scale
operators also ran services, including Kirby's
and Thorn's.

There were big changes too for the railways.

On 1 January 1948 the railway network was
nationalised and LNER became part of British
Railways. The UDC wasted no time in approaching
the new British Railways Commission to ask
for the line to be electrified.

Electrification from London to Shenfield did
indeed take place, in 1949, but it was to be
another five years before the Rayleigh branch
was electrified.

Work began in the summer of 1954 and
by 31 December 1956 all trains running on
the line were electric, with the exception of
the odd steam excursion. Electrification, of
course, led to more trains, which led to more

145 Rayleigh Library in the early 1960s, before it was replaced with the modern library building.

146 The interior of the old Rayleigh Library in the early 1960s.

commuting, which led to more development. Rayleigh's primary role from then until now has been as a commuter town.

From 1963 onwards some of the old signs of the past also disappeared as a result of the Beeching Report into railway rationalisation. Goods yards and other ancillary activities were phased out, goods traffic ceased and there is now no goods yard at Rayleigh.

1960s RE-DEVELOPMENT

As with many other places, Rayleigh saw much redevelopment in the 1960s. Many of the old, historic buildings in the town centre were swept away and replaced by functional, soulless concrete blocks. The wide open aspect of the High Street remained but the detail of the architecture was modern rather than traditional.

This caused some concern amongst local residents and in April 1963 a Rayleigh Civic Society was formed to arouse public interest in the retention of historic buildings and encourage good building and planning standards. Members were to have several major battles on their hands.

One of the many new buildings to be provided during this decade was the library. There had been much correspondence between the UDC and the County Council during the 1950s over the provision of new, purpose-

built library premises. In November 1952 'the Clerk reported that … the Branch Library which was previously situated at Barringtons [before the Council transferred there] moved to numbers 132-4 High Street, Rayleigh on Monday 13 October 1952'. This was the best arrangement yet for it, but the library was still being housed in converted premises. It took until 1965 for a purpose-built library (and accompanying social services offices) to be erected. A new police station and row of shops was erected opposite.

Also in 1965 the Council discussed the possibility of having a pedestrian precinct in Rayleigh but, no doubt with the impact on traffic in mind, decided against it.

Arguably the most controversial development proposal of the late 1960s was the application to demolish H. Mann & Sons, an ancient building occupying a prominent site. An inquiry found that the building 'formed a prominent, pleasing block of great architectural and historic interest … contributed to the street scene in closing the north part of the High Street and should be preserved'. It was also felt that 'a considerable and adequate programme of redevelopment was already underway in the town'. The decision to refuse demolition of the building was a landmark in 1960s redevelopment and for the conservation movement in Rayleigh.

147 The Mill Hall, built in the 1970s but pictured here in 2003 during refurbishment.

Developments which did take place included 33-37 High Street (next to the *White Horse*) and the site now occupied by Barclays Bank.

Meanwhile the area to the west of Mann's was radically remodelled in the 1970s, primarily with the widening and improvement of access to Bellingham Lane in mind. Round the corner another significant building would appear – the Mill Hall, opened on 1 October 1971.

By this stage Rayleigh was regarded as 'a major district shopping centre' with 'some land for residential development ... still available'. Although the population had already grown massively, a further 50 per cent increase was planned between 1961 and 1981. The predicted figure of 19,000 by 1971 was reached before that date, the population being made up mostly of commuters and young couples with children.

Outside the town, the Central Electricity Generating Board opened a large substation adjacent to the new spur road in what had been Rawreth parish. Lots of pylons began to appear on the local skyline.

THE END OF THE URBAN DISTRICT COUNCIL

Things were changing fast in 1960s Rayleigh, but one major change was to come from outside.

In the late-1960s the Local Government Commission announced that it was reviewing local government arrangements throughout the country and that it was likely that Rayleigh would be combined with another authority and lose its Urban District status and powers. This announcement met with almost universal displeasure in the town, but the machinery of government ground its way relentlessly to that end and in 1974 the UDC was abolished. Rochford Rural District Council was also abolished and Rayleigh was amalgamated with Rochford under a new Rochford District Council.

The 45-year period overseen by the UDC had been one of very rapid development. There had been great improvements in the housing stock and in leisure and recreation. Electricity use had become widespread, industry and services had expanded and there had been major growth in the District's population.

What was the next phase of the town's history to bring?

Ten

Modern Times

There was much opposition in Rayleigh at the time to the demise of the Urban District Council, as many felt that the town was somehow losing its identity. It was the largest town in the new Rochford District, yet it was not even mentioned by name in the District's title.

On the other hand, the Urban District had been carved out of the old Rochford Rural District, which itself had evolved from the old Rochford Hundred, so there might have been a sense that in some ways Rayleigh was returning to its roots.

Those in charge were wise enough to recognise the importance of Rayleigh both historically and as a key component of the modern District and decided to split some of the functions between Rochford and Rayleigh. This arrangement continues today, with Rochford being the administrative centre and Rayleigh the civic centre.

With Council offices already in existence in Rochford, the new Council decided to sell off the main Barringtons building but retain the extensions housing the Council chamber and Civic Suite. Council meetings still take place there.

The new Council was granted a coat-of-arms and a motto, 'Our Heritage, Our Future', and a reception for this took place on 5 May 1975 at the Mill Hall in Rayleigh. The coat-of-arms is topped by a representation of Rayleigh windmill.

DEVELOPMENT

Development continued apace under the new authority.

In 1975 work began on new Eastern Electricity Board offices in London Road (now occupied by Powergen). The company subsequently became a major employer in the town.

In the town centre, supermarkets had begun to appear. In 1978 International Stores took over Wallis before moving the following year to custom-built premises in Eastwood Road. The store was later taken over by Gateway and is now Somerfield. 1978 was also the year that Sainsbury's obtained planning permission to build on the old stadium site at Rayleigh Weir. An earlier town centre supermarket, Fine Fare, on the site of the old *Golden Lion*, subsequently saw service as a car showroom/motor accessory shop before being converted in 1976 into a nightclub, known for a long period as Crocs and now the Pink Toothbrush. Tesco also had a store in the High Street. It had opened in 1968.

Residential development continued to be focused on the western side of the town, on either side of London Road. Much of the land there had been in the ownership of the Ministry of Agriculture, Fisheries & Food (MAFF) since the 1950s and in 1984 the Council called a public meeting to outline development proposals for MAFF-owned land between London Road and Rawreth Lane. The plan was for 1,500 houses and an 80-acre public park. Over the next decade the houses were duly erected and Sweyne Park, attractively sited with views towards the church and windmill, was created.

Further areas of land at the Rawreth end of the town were subsequently earmarked for

148 Rawreth Lane, showing new housing development. This area of the town has greatly expanded in recent years.

development and from 1996 onwards planning applications began to be submitted. In total some 650 houses were proposed between Rawreth Lane and London Road, particularly around Victoria Avenue and Downhall Park Way. Houses are still being built in this area and the sale of Park School for redevelopment will further increase the number of new houses there.

Other areas identified for residential development in 1984 included land at Little Wheatley and at nearby Klondyke Avenue. With Rayleigh well-established as a commuter town, the latter development in particular was extremely well-placed, being right next to the railway station. Both sites have now been developed, focused around Bardfield Way/Langham Drive and Kestrel Grove respectively.

149 The new clinic in Rawreth Lane, shown here under construction and completed in 2004.

Permission to develop the Bardfield Way area had been given in the mid-1970s.

Other development has taken place around Daws Heath Road and there have been many infill developments of vacant plots, for example along Eastwood Road.

Town centre services were also improved under the new authority.

A new doctor's surgery was built on part of the King George's Field and in 1994 the Post Office moved its counter service from its building in the High Road to Martin's (now More), a more centrally placed facility.

1990 saw the commencement of Webster's Court, an office block in Webster's Way, and Burleigh House, built behind Kingsleigh House.

Outside the town centre a new industrial estate was growing up in Rawreth Lane and in 1993 a planning application was submitted for a large Macro warehouse there. A clause requesting the transaction of retail sales at the warehouse caused great concern to High Street shopkeepers, who feared a serious impact on their businesses. However, this element was withdrawn from the final submission and wholesale sales only were permitted. Construction of the warehouse duly went ahead.

The development at the former Park School site includes the provision of a new multi-million-pound sports centre, planned to open during 2005. This will include a sports hall, squash courts, an aerobic studio, a gym, outdoor football pitches and a skateboard facility.

TRAFFIC AND PUBLIC TRANSPORT

More and more cars continued to appear on local roads and further initiatives were tried to help traffic flow.

Outside the town centre one major scheme placed on the drawing board in 1985 was the construction of an underpass at Rayleigh Weir, which was becoming seriously congested. Previous proposals for an overpass in the early 1970s had been strongly opposed, but traffic levels had increased so much that it was becoming imperative that something was done. An underpass was seen as having a less detrimental effect on nearby residents and with sufficient impetus this time to see it through the underpass was duly constructed. It was formally opened on Thursday 19 December 1991.

In 1988 Essex County Council launched a major transport initiative, the South East Essex Traffic Study, to seek ways to reduce traffic congestion in the districts of Southend, Rochford and Castle Point (an amalgamation of the old Benfleet Urban District Council with the old Canvey Island Urban District Council). Rayleigh, historically the road gateway to these areas and a fundamental node in the modern-day local traffic network, featured heavily and an exhibition of proposals was held in April 1989 at the Mill Hall.

Areas identified for immediate short-term improvement included Bedloes Corner, the *Carpenters Arms* roundabout, the A130 at Battlesbridge, plus various major road junctions such as Rawreth Lane/Hullbridge Road and Hambro Hill/Hockley Road. The widespread introduction of mini-roundabouts was initiated throughout the study area.

Amongst the schemes considered for further investigation were the widening of the A127 to three lanes in each direction and the construction of an outer bypass for Rayleigh, Hockley, Hawkwell, Ashingdon and Rochford, with local connections to the existing road network. Neither scheme came to fruition.

150　The old Park School site in 2004, awaiting redevelopment for leisure and residential purposes.

One scheme rejected on environmental and economic grounds was a proposal for an inner bypass for Rayleigh, Hockley and Hawkwell, running to the south of Hockley Woods and costing £28 million.

Although no outer bypass has yet been built, the idea for it is periodically refloated.

The South East Essex Traffic Study also included measures to improve public transport in the area. Amongst the more ambitious proposals was one for a light railway linking Canvey Island to Shoeburyness via Rayleigh and Eastwood. This, too, was never built.

On the roads, there were proposals for giving priority to buses, which had coincidentally been deregulated in October 1986, increasing competition. The town is now served by Arriva and First. Whilst there are still no buses-only lanes in Rayleigh the town remains a major stopping point in the south-east Essex bus network. Rayleigh station is the western terminus of routes 1, 7 and 9, all of which link the town with Southend. Many other buses to places as disparate as Stansted, Chelmsford and Basildon pass through the town.

HERITAGE AND ENVIRONMENTAL AWARENESS

Despite, or perhaps because of, the continued development, the 1970s onwards saw a growing awareness of heritage and environmental issues in the town.

In 1969 Essex County Council had approved a conservation area covering the town centre,

151   An aerial view of the Rayleigh Weir underpass under construction.

a significant sign that concerns over the loss of some of the town's ancient buildings were being taken seriously. This incorporated Rayleigh Mount, Holy Trinity Church, Barringtons, the King George's Field, the High Street and Crown Hill.

Nevertheless, occasional threats to Rayleigh's built heritage continued to manifest themselves, but the presumption in the case of significant historic buildings tended now to be in favour of their retention rather than their demolition. For example, in early 1980 Barringtons Cottages were threatened with demolition, but planning permission for this was refused.

One building which did go was the old *Regal* cinema, although the loss was sweetened a little by the opportunity which its demolition presented in the early 1980s for further archaeological investigations of what was once part of the outer bailey of Rayleigh Castle.

Homeregal House was built on the cinema site in the late 1980s.

Another loss was initiated in 1985 when a proposal was submitted to demolish 57-61 High Street, three Edwardian houses with shops built onto their fronts. Although these were not especially important there was much local opposition to their proposed demolition as they were the last shops of their kind on the eastern side of the High Street. After a short campaign and a series of revised planning applications, approval was nevertheless given to demolish them and they were replaced in 1993 by what is now Steeple High.

Although the Edwardian buildings were lost, the town's architectural watchdogs, the Civic Society, welcomed the look of their replacement as being an improvement on similar previous constructions, observing that 'the architectural style of this building is a great improvement on

152 Crown Hill, showing new development and traffic congestion, two sides of life in modern-day Rayleigh.

the brutal style of the 1960s, examples of which can be seen in other parts of the High Street'.

On the plus side, Wern Cottages were refurbished in 1985, having fallen into disrepair despite being listed. The same year saw a successful campaign to retain a traditional red telephone box outside the *Crown*. Next to it stands an original King George VI postbox, which was transferred to Rochford District Council from Royal Mail Anglia in 1994 in return for the payment of a single red rose.

1986 saw nationwide celebrations for the 900th anniversary of Domesday Book, in which Rayleigh Castle is mentioned. This provided another reminder for Rayleigh residents that they had much of historic interest in their midst that should be retained.

This cause was helped too in 1989 with Essex Heritage Year. To mark this, Rochford District Council held a competition for the design of parish signs within its administrative area and the Rayleigh sign, which now stands in the High Street opposite Crown Hill and features four of the principal historic buildings in the town (Rayleigh Mount, Holy Trinity

Church, the Dutch Cottage and the windmill), was designed by the Rayleigh Civic Society. The wooden post which supports it was carved from a tree from Hockley Woods.

In 1997 a planning application was lodged for the demolition of Brooklands in Hockley Road, which had been used from the 1950s to the mid-1990s by the Essex Education Committee, and for its replacement with a block of retirement homes. The building had a distinctive facade and there was much interest locally in trying at the very least to get the facade retained. Some of the land around it had been sold off for development over a decade earlier and now the building itself was under threat. After discussions, a compromise was reached whereby the developer agreed to recreate the facade of the old building in the new one and the retirement homes development duly took place. Brooklands Public Gardens, on land to the immediate north of the building, was opened in 1978.

Since the Millennium the area around Rayleigh windmill has been greatly improved, following the demolition of an old mill building, the provision of increased car parking and improvements to landscaping.

Concerns also turned in the late 1970s and 1980s to the need to protect the natural environment. By this stage much land around Rayleigh and Rawreth had been designated as Green Belt. In 1977 a large area of countryside to the east of the town on the lower slopes of the Rayleigh Hills was designated as the Roach Valley Conservation Zone. These designations have helped to protect much of the natural environment around the town over the past 30 years.

RELIGION

At Holy Trinity Church, the Rev. Hatch continued to serve until 1982. He died in 1993 and his ashes are interred in the churchyard outside the church's east wall. He was succeeded in 1983 by the Rev. Peter Taylor.

During the Rev. Taylor's incumbency HRH Princess Anne visited Holy Trinity for the Missions to Seamen Fair on 27 April 1988 to mark 35 years of the Rayleigh Branch of the Missions to Seamen, the princess being the president of the national organisation. This period also saw the establishment of Grovewood church at Grove Junior School in Grove Road.

The Rev. Taylor was succeeded in 1996 by the Rev. David Parrott. The Reverend Parrott left in 2004 to take up a post as Continuing Ministerial Education Officer for Chelmsford Diocese. At the time of writing a new incumbent is awaited.

Meanwhile, the future of the old Parish Rooms looked uncertain. Closed in 1976 following the erection of the new Parish Hall behind the church, they stood empty and abandoned while various ideas came and went about what to do with them. Despite being listed, they suffered serious vandalism and there was even talk of their demolition. However, in 1981 the building was purchased by two local businessmen, restored and opened as Amigo's restaurant. By the turn of the 21st century things had come full circle and the restaurant is now closed and the building unused.

In 1979 the Catholic Church opened its own Parish Hall in London Road, named in honour of Pope John Paul II.

The 1970s also saw a proposal to demolish the Baptist Church, a listed 18th-century building which was beginning to show its age. However, permission to demolish it was fortunately refused and the building was duly restored and reopened in 1981. A large, complementary extension was built on the north side as part of the improvement works.

Elsewhere, the Jehovah's Witnesses have a new hall on the former gasworks land in Crown Hill and a modern-style Community Church exists at the Warehouse Centre in Brook Road.

TOWN COUNCIL

Under the 1974 reorganisation Rochford District Council became the first tier of local government for Rayleigh citizens. However, it did not go unnoticed in the town that several communities in the District were supported at a local level by their own parish councils, the first point of call for local issues. The new District Council did operate a Rayleigh Consultative Committee, but this was still controlled from Rochford and local people wanted self-government from Rayleigh again. The town, bigger than most, began to put its case for having a local council of its own once more.

Several attempts were made during the 1980s and early 1990s to get a local council established for Rayleigh, but each time the application was rejected by the Boundary Commission.

Rochford District Council had never been very interested in the establishment of a Town Council for Rayleigh, but by the mid-1990s things were happening on a wider plane under a Local Government Commission review into the possible creation of unitary authorities and the Council now began to warm to the idea, if it could be proved that there was sufficient demand for it amongst Rayleigh residents.

Finally, in 1995, the Commission granted permission for a new Rayleigh Town Council to be formed. The first elections were held in May 1996 and the Council now provides the first level of local authority support for Rayleigh residents.

TOWN LIFE

Town life in post-1974 Rayleigh saw several celebrations.

First, in 1977, there was Queen Elizabeth II's Silver Jubilee, celebrated by a week-long fair with various musical attractions and sideshows. This was followed in 2002 by her Golden Jubilee, which was marked amongst other things by the creation of a small garden on the King George's Field.

In addition to Princess Anne's visit to Holy Trinity, 1988 saw a second major event when Rayleigh took part in the 'Fire Over England' celebrations in July to mark the 400th anniversary of the defeat of the Spanish Armada. This took the form of the lighting of a national chain of beacons in imitation of the method used at the time for sending signals around the country. Rayleigh, with its hilltop location, was an ideal town to take part in this event. It had featured in the original 1588 chain of beacons used to alert the country to the presence of the Armada, but the original site on Rayleigh Mount could not be used as it was now a protected ancient monument.

The new beacon, in Bellingham Lane, in front of the Mill Hall, was lit by Councillor Roy Pearson, Chairman of Rochford District Council, at precisely 10.21pm, the time designated for the lighting of all 23 Essex beacons in the chain. It was one of more than 200 nationwide and was one of many built to the original ancient specification, taking the form of a fuel-filled iron brazier mounted on an 18-feet-high pole.

The beacon lighting ceremony was preceded by an open-air production of *The Taming of the Shrew*, performed on nearby Rayleigh Mount by the Southend Shakespeare Company, and the reading of Queen Elizabeth I's famous 'Tilbury Speech' (the words spoken by the Queen to her troops at Tilbury). The bells of Holy Trinity were also sounded to mark the event.

The beacon has since been lit to mark the Millennium and Queen Elizabeth II's Golden Jubilee.

153 The beacon in front of the Mill Hall, which was one of a chain of such beacons across the country used to mark the 400th anniversary in 1988 of the defeat of the Spanish Armada.

Another event designed to mark the Millennium was the erection of a town clock at Mann's Corner, unveiled by Rayleigh Town Council chairman, Councillor Jeanette Helson, in November 1999. A time capsule was buried at the foot of the clock on 31 December 1999. It is scheduled to be opened after 50 years.

The centrepiece of the Millennium celebrations was a festival weekend in April 2000, which featured events which had become traditional in the town for such occasions, such as sports, music, crafts and a religious service on King George's Field.

Subsequent celebrations in the town have included regular awards in the Britain in Bloom competitions.

CURRENT ISSUES

The increasing development and the traffic which it brings have given the County, District and Town Councils much food for thought. The 1988 South East Essex Traffic Study

154   Rayleigh town centre from Holy Trinity Church, showing how it looked in 2004.

predicted traffic growth of 75 per cent in the study area by 2006.

In 1997 the one-way system in the town centre was replaced by two-way working in Webster's Way in an attempt to ease traffic flow. However, it is questionable whether this scheme has been entirely successful, as queues still regularly form in Crown and London Hills, High, Hockley and Eastwood Roads and Webster's Way. Rayleigh occupies a central position in the local road network and to get from Hockley in the north to the Weir in the south, or from the *Carpenter's Arms* in the west to Eastwood in the east, the most direct route is through the town centre. It is often quicker to walk up Crown Hill or along Webster's Way than to drive.

Add to this the increasing congestion around the shopping centre at the Weir and 21st-century Rayleigh must surely be a candidate for one of the worst traffic-congested towns in Essex.

The opening of the southern section of a new A130 bypass to the west of the town in February 2003 has reduced congestion on what is now the old A130, but this is only

one measure in an area that needs many more. £700,000 of Thames Gateway money was made available in 2004 for improvements to Webster's Way. This money is due to be spent in 2005 but the project is more about improving the environment of this road which faces the backs of High Street properties rather than about improving traffic flow.

The local press continues to be filled with letters from residents volunteering suggestions for improvement. Some of these have advocated a reversion to two-way traffic in the High Street. Many more have proposed the construction of new roads to remove the need to go through the town centre. However, the real issue is that we are wedded to the car and until incentives or penalties are introduced to radically alter car usage the underlying problem will not go away. It is time to grasp the nettle and Rayleigh would be a good town to start with.

CONCLUSIONS

Rayleigh has come a long way since the first human visitors arrived on Hambro Hill in the Stone Age. After periods of prosperity and

155 Millennium celebrations in Rayleigh. The clock in the photograph was built to commemorate the event.

decline, and still predominantly rural as recently as 1889, it has been transformed by the arrival of the railway and subsequent 20th-century development into a bustling commuter town. On the map it marks the western extent of the urban area of south-east Essex centred on Southend. The population in 2001 was over 30,000.

Much former agricultural land has been swallowed up and yet in contrast many planned 20th-century schemes for development have only partially been carried out. For example, in the west, off Rawreth Lane, land between Madrid Avenue and Hooley Drive retains much plotland character, as does land in the east around Lancaster and Connaught Roads, The Drive and Rayleigh Downs Road. In the north, Wellington Road has only been partly built and ends in fields, whilst nearby Napier Road is still just a track. Land in some of these areas now provides an important habitat for urban wildlife, such as Grove Woods at the northern end of Lancaster and Connaught Roads which is a mixture of native and introduced plant species and provides a reminder of plotland life in the first half of the 20th century.

Outside the busy centre there is still much green land around the town, and even in the centre major areas such as King George's Field complement the historic buildings to give Rayleigh the feel of a bustling, semi-rural market town.

Rayleigh has experienced periods of regional and national significance and, despite its many modern services, retains a heritage of old buildings and a surrounding natural landscape of which any town would be proud. And that hilltop location, with its views over the surrounding countryside, really is a joy!

'It is an unusual sensation in Essex or East Anglia,' wrote the local historian Norman Scarfe about Rayleigh, 'to be in a small town centre perched up well above 200 feet.'

He might well have added that the sensation is also a delightful one, as any visitor will testify as he makes his way along the High Street and the High Road exploring his surroundings.

Select Bibliography

The items listed below were extremely useful in the research for this book.

A Guide to Southend by a Gentleman (1824)

Addison, William, *Essex Worthies* (1973)

Babbington, Terry, *Thundersley – A Pictorial History* (1993)

Beer, Noel, *A Glimpse of 19th-century Rayleigh from Events at the Lion Inn* (1999)

Beer, Noel, *An Annotated Bibliography of Rayleigh* (2003 edition)

Beer, Noel, *Education in 19th-century Rayleigh* (2001)

Beer, Noel, *Health Care in Early 19th-century Rayleigh* (2001)

Beer, Noel, *Law & Order in 19th-century Rayleigh* (2000)

Beer, Noel, *Leisure & Entertainment in 19th-century Rayleigh* (2002)

Beer, Noel, *Turnpike Roads Around Rayleigh* (2000)

Beer, Noel, *When the Railway Came to Rayleigh* (2003)

Benton, Philip, *The History of Rochford Hundred* (1867-88 [1991 reprint])

Brake, George Thompson, *The History of the Methodist Church in the Southend and Leigh Circuit – Rayleigh* (1994)

Brake, George Thompson, *The Scene of Early Methodism in the Rochford Hundred* (1994)

Burrows, J.W., *Southend-on-Sea & District* (1909 [1970 reprint])

Clack, Edward, *Spy in the Sky* (1992)

Clarke, Michael, *Rochford Hall* (1990)

Cooke, George Alexander, *Topographical & Statistical Description of the County of Essex* (*c.*1810)

Cross, Doug, *Rayleigh Baptist Church – The Fourth Jubilee* (1998)

Crump, R.W., *91 Rayleigh High Street* (1991)

Delahoy, Richard, *Eastern National* (2003)

Delahoy, Richard, *Southend Corporation Transport* (1986)

Department of the Environment, *List of Buildings of Special Architectural or Historical Interest – Rochford District* (1986)

Dilley, Roy, *The Dream Palaces of Southend* (1983)

Eastern National Omnibus Company Limited, *Eastern National – Fifty Years of Service* 1930-80 (1980)

Eddy, M.R., 'Dutch Cottages in Essex' from *Essex Archaeology and History*, 3rd Series, Vol 22, pages 122-31 (1991)

Eddy, M.R. and Petchey, M.R., *Historic Towns in Essex – An Archaeological Survey of Saxon and Medieval towns, with guidance for their future planning* (1983)

Edwards, A.C., *A History of Essex* (1985)

Ellis, Clarence, *Hubert de Burgh – A Study In Constancy* (1952)

English, Jacqueline A., *The Dutch Cottage, Crown Hill, Rayleigh* (undated, but *c.*1980s)

Essex County Council, *Origins of Rayleigh* (1993)

Essex Society for Family History, *Monumental Inscriptions at Holy Trinity Church and Churchyard, Rayleigh, Essex* (1992)

Feather, Fred, *The Rayleigh Bath-chair Murder* (undated leaflet, but *c.*1990s)

Fletcher, Reg, *Christchurch United Reformed Church, Rayleigh* (1998)

Francis, E.B., 'Rayleigh Castle: New Facts in its History and Recent Explorations on its site' article in the *Transactions of the Essex Archaeological Society* (1910)

Farries, K.G., *Essex Windmills, Millers and Millwrights – Volume IV* (1985)

Fryer, Rev. A.G., *Rayleigh in Past Days* (1908)

Fryer, Rev. A.G., *Rayleigh Yesterday & Today* (1932)

Gifford, P.R. (Ed.), *Resist the Invader* (1982)

Gifford, P.R. (Ed.), *'the maize, the wheat and the rye'* (1979)

Granville, Dr. A.B., *Spas of England* (1841)

Helliwell, Leonard, *South East Essex in the Saxon Period* (1971)

Helliwell, L. and MacLeod, D.G., *Rayleigh Castle* (1981)

Holland, Michael, 'Guilty As Charged' in *Essex Harvest* (2003)

Holmes, J.H. and Newton, K.C., *Highways & Byways of Essex* (1955)

Hough, John, *Essex Churches* (1983)

Hunter, John, *The Essex Landscape* (1999)

Jacobs, Norman, *Speedway in East Anglia* (2000)

Jarvis, Stan, *Essex Murder Casebook* (1994)

Jerram-Burrows, L.E., *Bygone Rochford* (1988)

Jerram-Burrows, L.E., *Smugglers' Moon* (1993)

Johnson, L.J., *The Posts of Essex* (1969)

Kelly's Directory (various)

King, H.W., 'The Lawless Court of the Honor of Rayleigh' article in the *Transactions of the Essex Archaeological Society* (1891)

Lane, Ernest H., *Rayleigh – Its People and Places* (1996)

Lane, Ernest H. and Fitzgerald, Edward, *Rayleigh – A Pictorial History* (1991)

Laver, Henry, 'Rayleigh Mount – A British Oppidum' article in the *Transactions of the Essex Archaeological Society* (1891)

MacLeod, Donald G., *South East Essex in the Prehistoric Period* (1971)

Mason, Rev. Thomas W., *Royal and Romantic Rayleigh* [a pageant] (1925)

Medlycott, Maria, *Rayleigh Historic Towns Project Assessment Report* (1998)

Morant, Philip, *The History & Antiquities of the County of Essex* (1768 [1978 reprint])

Morris, John (Ed.), *Domesday Book – Essex* (1086 [1983 reprint])

Mrs Johnson's Rayleigh Scrapbook (a collection of newspaper cuttings from the 18th and 19th centuries)

Neale, Kenneth, *Essex – 'full of profitable thinges'* (1996)

Neale, Kenneth, *Essex in History* (1977)

Newton, R.I., *Holy Trinity, Rayleigh – Some Rectors* (1934)

Pevsner, Nikolaus, *The Buildings of England – Essex* (1988 [reprint])

Phillips, Charles, *The Shenfield to Southend Line* (1984)

Pollitt, William, *Southend Before the Norman Conquest* (1953)

Post Office Directory of Essex (1866)

Rackham, Oliver, *The Woods of South-East Essex* (1986)

Rayleigh Civic Society, *Over The Years* (1997)

Rayleigh Civic Society, *Up & Down the High Street – Historical Guide to Rayleigh High Street* (2002 edition)

Rayleigh Martyrs' Memorial – Programme of the Ceremony of Unveiling (1908)

Rayleigh Mount Local Committee of the National Trust, *Rayleigh Mount* (1965)

Rayleigh Parish Registers

Rayleigh Parish Vestry Minutes

Rayleigh Town Council, *Rayleigh 2000* (2000)

Rayleigh Urban District Council Minutes

Reaney, P.H., *The Place-names of Essex* (1969)

Reaney, P.H., 'The Place-names of Rochford Hundred' in the *Transactions of the Southend & District Antiquarian & Historical Society* (1932)

Rodwell, Warwick, *South East Essex in the Roman Period* (1971)

Royal Commission on Historic Monuments (Volume IV – South East Essex) (1923)

Salmon, Nathaniel, *The History & Antiquities of Essex* (1740)

Scarfe, Norman, *Essex* (1975)

Scollan, Maureen, *Sworn to Serve* (1993)
Simpson, F.D. and Clark, P.F., *The Bridge Family & Its Buses* (1983)
Skinner, Charlotte, *Caley of Rayleigh* (1914)
Smith, J.R., *The Speckled Monster* (1987)
Smith, Ken, *Essex Under Arms* (1998)
Snell, Peter J., *Westcliff-on-Sea Motor Services Ltd.* (1987)
Sorrell, Mark, *The Peculiar People* (1979)
Strutt, Robert John, *John William Strutt, 3rd Baron Rayleigh* (1924)
The Field Lane Story (author and date unknown)
The Fitzwimarc School 1937-87 (1987)
Turpin, B.J. and J.M., *Windmills in Essex* (1977)
Victoria County History (Volumes I-X) (1903–2001)
Vingoe, Lesley, *Hockley, Hullbridge and Hawkwell Past* (1999)
Walker, Leonard, *Background to Domesday* (1988)
Walker, Wendy, *Essex Markets & Fairs* (1981)
Weever, John, *Funeral Monuments* (1631)
White, William, *Directory of Essex* (1848)
Woodgate, John, *The Essex Police* (1985)
Wright, Thomas, *The History of the County of Essex* (1834)
Yearsley, Ian, *A History of Southend* (2001)
Yearsley, Ian, *Essex Events* (1999)
Yearsley, Ian, *Hadleigh Past* (1998)
Yearsley, Ian, *The Essex Skyline* (manuscript, 1994)

Apart from the books listed above, the following were also extremely useful …

Guidebooks to the following churches: Holy Trinity, Baptist, Rayleigh Tabernacle, Congregational Church/United Reformed Church, including *Rayleigh Congregational Church Golden Jubilee Anniversary* 1910-1960.

Various issues of the following magazines and newspapers: *East Anglian Daily Times, Essex Chronicle, Essex Countryside, Kent & Essex Mercury, Rayleigh Times*.

Various items from the *Transactions* of the Essex Archaeological Society.

Documentation about 'The Asplin Family of Little Wakering' (including biographical information about, and the diary of, Dr Jonas Asplin) held at the Essex Record Office.

The Scheduled Ancient Monument listing for Rayleigh from the Department of Culture, Media and Sport.

Rochford District Council town guide and town planning brochures.

Documents and photographs held by Southend Museums Service and the Essex Record Office.

Maps from all periods were indispensable, including those of Christopher Saxton (1576), John Norden (1594) and Chapman & André (1777), plus the Tithe Map for Rayleigh (1841) and various editions of Ordnance Survey maps.

Various auction and sale particulars.

Information in the museum at Rayleigh windmill and the talks programme of the Historical Society of Rayleigh, which looks after it. Rayleigh Historical Society and Rayleigh Town Council historical information signs throughout Rayleigh. National Trust information boards at Rayleigh Mount.

Index

References which relate to illustrations only are given in **bold**.

RAYLEIGH, ESSEX

Seven miles from Westcliff and the important County Borough of Southend-on-Sea. A Picturesque RESIDENTIAL PROPERTY and about 25 ACRES OF FREEHOLD LAND suitable for immediate development as BUILDING ESTATES affording many eligible Sites for the erection of small but attractive Residences which are in great and increasing demand in this healthy and pleasant locality. The whole of the property is within a few minutes of Rayleigh Station on the London & North Eastern Railway with a good service of trains to and from the City.

Particulars and Conditions of Sale

of the

ATTRACTIVE RESIDENCE

known as

"Rayleigh House"

Approached by a carriage drive from the Main Road, occupying a high and healthy situation, commanding magnificent views. The matured and delightful Gardens and Pleasure Grounds extend to an area of nearly

SEVEN ACRES

with Orchards and walled-in Kitchen Garden. In the Grounds are a wealth of Matured Ornamental Trees and Flowering Shrubs. A range of

GLASSHOUSES, STABLING, MOTOR HOUSES and ENTRANCE LODGE

Held upon Lease for an unexpired term of about 43 years at a Ground Rent of £41 : 10 : 0 per annum.

Vacant Possession will be given on Completion of the Purchase.

Also in Two Lots, The Valuable and Eligible

FREEHOLD LAND

Adjoining the Grounds of "Rayleigh House" and adjacent to Rayleigh Station having a total area of about

TWENTY-FIVE ACRES

with valuable frontages to High Street, Wheatleys Road, Love Lane and the main Chelmsford-Southend Road, and well adapted for development as

BUILDING ESTATES

Upon a portion of the Land is the Freehold Detached Cottage known as "SANDPIT COTTAGE," with Large Garden.

For Sale by Auction by

Messrs. TALBOT & WHITE

At their ESTATE SALE ROOM—*No. 34 CLARENCE STREET, Southend-on-Sea*

On SATURDAY, JUNE 23rd, 1928, at 3.30 in the afternoon precisely.

Printed Particulars with Plans and Conditions of Sale may be obtained of

The Solicitors—

Messrs. ASHURST, MORRIS, CRISP & Co.
17 Throgmorton Avenue, London, E.C. 2.

W. BYGOTT Esqr.—*Solicitor*
High Street, Rayleigh, Essex.

The Auctioneers—

Messrs. TALBOT & WHITE { 34 Clarence Street, Southend-on-Sea, and
29 Hamlet Court Road, Westcliff-on-Sea.

Telephone—Southend-on-Sea 37.